The Wit and Wisdom of G. K. Chesterton

The Wit and Wisdom of G. K. Chesterton

Selected and introduced by

BEVIS HILLIER

continuum

Continuum International Publishing Group
The Tower Building, 11 York Road, London SE1 7NX
80 Maiden Lane, Suite 704, New York NY 10038

www.continuumbooks.com

First published 2010

British Library Cataloguing-in-Publication Data
A catalogue record for this book is available from the British Library.

ISBN 978-1-4411-7958-6

Designed and typeset by Kenneth Burnley, Wirral, Cheshire
Printed and bound by the MPG Books Group

CONTENTS

Dedications

T O R I C H A

R D I N G R A

M S W H O S H

A R E S S O M

E O F G K C H

E S T E R T O

N S M O R E U

N O R T H O D

O X V I E W S

B Y H O O K O

R B Y C R O O

K I A M F I R

S T W I T H T

H I S B O O K

and

T O J O H N A N

D A N N H E A L

D W I T H T H A

N K S F O R A L

L T H E I R H E

L P A N D A D V

I C E T H I S I

S T H E F I R S

T O F T W O B O

O K S I A M D E

D I C A T I N G

T O T H E M I N

T H I S M I L L

E N N I U M G U

L F S D I V I D

E W R I T E R S

L I K E O R W E

L L A N D C H E

S T E R T O N B

U T B O T H W E

R E G E N I U S

E S W E R E N T

T H E Y Q U A L

I T Y W I L L A

L W A Y S O U T

and

T O D O

N A L D

W I N T

E R S G

I L L A

F R I E

N D O F

M O R E

T H A N

F O R T

Y Y E A

R S H E

K I N D

L Y R E

A D T H

E P R O

O F S O

F T H I

S B O O

K A N D

S U G G

E S T E

D S O M

E H E A

D I N G

S B E T

T E R T

H A N T

H O S E

I H A D

I N V E

N T E D

I A L S

O S E N

D M Y L

O V E T

O H I S

W I F E

M A R Y

INTRODUCTION

G. K. Chesterton was a man who thought in epigrams. When I approached the publisher of this book to suggest an anthology of Chesterton's writings, I said: 'I'm sure there's already some dinky "Wit and Wisdom" book; but I want to do the thing properly.' To my surprise, when I checked in the London Library, I found no such compilation. There was a book of 1875 of *The Wit and Wisdom of the Earl of Chesterfield*, but nothing on Chesterton. D. B. Wyndham Lewis, co-compiler of *The Stuffed Owl* book of bad verse, had produced a Chesterton anthology, but it was of *complete* stories, essays and poems – not, as in the present book, of short quotations, or 'gobbets'. W. H. Auden had similarly used extended extracts in *G. K. Chesterton: A Selection from his Non-Fictional Prose* (he had no stomach for Chesterton's novels, which tend to be allegorical farragoes). And P. J. Kavanagh had also used long quotations in *The Bodley Head G. K. Chesterton*.

But I was right. A trawl of the British Library catalogue showed that there had indeed been a dinky anthology of GKC. *Wit and Wisdom of G. K. Chesterton* had been published in 1911. It therefore omitted a quarter of a century of his best writing; it contained only six quotations from GKC's *The Illustrated London News* columns, which are such a staple of the present book. (It was reissued in New York in 2002 as *Chesterton Day by Day*, each quotation being assigned to a particular day of the year.) It was no competition to the much more extensive anthology I had in mind.

As early as 1948, Marshall McLuhan had made the case for such a book. In his Introduction to Hugh Kenner's *Paradox in Chesterton* he wrote:

> It is important . . . that a Chesterton anthology should be made along the lines indicated by Mr Kenner. Not an anthology which preserves the Victorian flavour of his journalism by extensive quotation, but one of short excerpts which would permit the reader to feel Chesterton's powerful intrusion into every kind of confused moral and psychological issue of our time.

Actually, if you read Kenner's book, you find no suggestion that a Chesterton anthology should be undertaken: the idea was entirely McLuhan's, as Kenner wrily indicated at the beginning of his Notes.★

Just under twenty years later, in 1967, McLuhan published his influential book *The Medium is the Message*; and if ever there was a writer for whom that could be claimed, it was Chesterton, whose poetry and prose are instinct with his worship of robustness.

Again in the 1960s, Malcolm Muggeridge also urged that somebody should corral Chesterton aphorisms:

> Chesterton's most notable talent was for the sudden crystallization of illuminating observations. It would be a good idea . . . to make a collection of these, like La Rochefoucauld's *Maximes*.

But neither McLuhan nor Muggeridge followed his own prescription. I have done so, though not because of their advocacy.

A curious occurrence put the idea of a Chesterton book into my head. I live in a medieval almshouse in Winchester, the

---

★'Pending the compilation of such a Chesterton anthology as is projected in the Introduction [by Marshall McLuhan], these notes are offered as assistance to the reader . . .'

Hospital of St Cross. (It was founded by William the Conqueror's grandson about 1132, and is the setting of Anthony Trollope's 1855 novel, *The Warden*.) As a Grade I listed building it is open to the public. In the summer season a cafeteria is run by ladies from the neighbourhood, who give their help for free.

One day in 2007 I was coming back from a shopping trip in the city, which lies about a mile from the almshouse. As I walked through the high Gothic arch that leads into the Hospital – architecture exactly described by Trollope at the beginning of his novel – an elderly lady flew out of the cafeteria.

'Mr Hillier?' she asked. I pleaded guilty.

'Would you sign my copy of your Betjeman biography?'

Of course I said I would be delighted to do so, and joined her for coffee. She introduced herself as Mrs Nancy Dixon.

During the conversation, she told me that her mother, Frederica [Freda] Spencer (later Mrs Bayley), had been secretary to G. K. Chesterton early in the First World War in Beaconsfield and that she, Nancy, owned many letters from him to her mother and a number of his accomplished drawings and caricatures. Would I like to borrow them?

I did so, and found the letters spirited and witty. They were nearly all in his handwriting, which someone uncharitable might call 'mannered'; I would rather describe it as 'characterful'. It was clear that GKC had a bit of a crush on Freda (though in no dirty old man way); the tone of many of the letters was flirtatious as well as facetious. Some of the drawings were brilliant. One was a caricature of Winston Churchill, *c.* 1919, which has never been reproduced until now (Illustration 1).

Reading Chesterton's sparkling letters to Nancy Dixon's mother sent me back to his novels and poetry. Looking him up in the *Oxford Dictionary of National Biography*, I learned that he had died in 1936. That meant that he had just gone out of copyright – copyright in a writer's works persists for 70 years after his or her death. To put it crudely, it was open season on Chesterton.

Illustration 1: Caricature of Winston Churchill by Chesterton. *British Library.*

It happened that I had three other tenuous links with GKC. In the early 1930s, as a schoolgirl, my mother, *née* Mary Louise Palmer, had won a national essay competition for schools. It was judged by Chesterton and he presented her with her prize – a portable 'Imperial' typewriter (on which I learned to type as a child).

Second, I knew that GKC had contributed a weekly column to *The Illustrated London News* from 1905 until his death in 1936. In 1962, about to leave Oxford, I had been interviewed for a job on that magazine by its editor, Sir Bruce Ingram. Thanks partly to nepotism, he had been editor *since Queen Victoria's reign* (1900) and was therefore the man who had commissioned and published all of GKC's columns. When I entered the old man's office I said: 'Good morning, sir.'

'Good morning, sir,' he replied – a courtesy unheard of at that date from an older man to a young one. Very Dickensian, I thought.

The interview did not go well. I later realized that Ingram was a collector of English watercolours (he wrote a book on the genre), and if we could have touched on that subject, I might have scored some marks. As it was, he asked me: 'Have you gone in for sports at Oxford, Mr Hillier?'

'Well,' I said, aware that my reply was going to sound a little absurd, 'I did play croquet for my college.'

'I meant *field* sports,' Ingram growled.

At the end of the interview he said: 'If you want to be a journalist, Mr Hillier, you will have to learn to be accurate. I see you have dated your letter "September 31st".' I didn't get the job.

My third link with GKC was that I was a friend of his godson, the cartoonist Nicolas Bentley – the son of his lifelong friend, Edmund Clerihew Bentley. Nicolas and I ran a dining-and-debate club within the Garrick Club, the 'Unreasonables'.

Reading Chesterton, I saw that his works – more, perhaps, than those of any writer since Dr Johnson – lent themselves to, if I may invent a word not yet in the *Oxford English Dictionary*, 'gobbetization' – the plucking out of witty, funny, mischievous, controversial, sometimes profound gobbets. (Most of the extracts in this book are brief; but just occasionally I have given him freer rein.)

Following the encounter with Nancy Dixon which put me on the Chesterton trail, there were two more unexpected coincidences. Chesterton is perhaps best known as the father of Father Brown; and in a *Spectator* article of 19–26 December 2009, Sinclair McKay pointed out that 2010 would mark the 100th anniversary of the first appearance of GKC's perspicacious priest. McKay wrote:

A chap murdered by an invisible man? A decapitated Scottish laird with the fillings stolen from his skull? A poet, hypnotized into committing suicide? Who could deal with such curious and baffling crimes?

There's only one possible answer: an amateur sleuth who specialized in the bizarre and diabolical long before Mulder and Scully; a detective long due for a comeback: G. K. Chesterton's Father Brown.

Although the 52 short stories in which he featured never go out of print, this stumpy black-clad figure with his umbrella, face 'like a Norfolk dumpling' and passionate outbursts of anger in the face of dumb superstition, is weirdly neglected today. Why, for instance, is Father Brown not a part of that eternal ITV Holmes/Poirot/Marple television detective roster? It's Father Brown's 100th anniversary this coming year, and it's about time he became a proper TV star.

In 1910, when the first *Father Brown* tales were published, G. K. Chesterton was already a literary whirlwind, a ferociously energetic writer who disguised his true depth with Technicolor prose.

Some of Chesterton's novels, such as *The Man Who Was Thursday*, perhaps do not hold up so well now. But *The Father Brown Stories* were, in their own modest way, works of genius. Influential, too: Evelyn Waugh and Alfred Hitchcock were among their eager followers. One of Father Brown's quotes is used as the title of book three of *Brideshead Revisited* – 'A Twitch upon the Thread'.

The other Chestertonian eye-opener came when I mentioned to Sean Hawkins that I was compiling a GKC anthology. Sean used to own the Ancient House Bookshop (now sadly closed down) in my home town of Reigate, Surrey. 'Oh,' he said, 'in that case I must show you some photographs I have of Chesterton and his mother when he was a boy.' These, which have never been reproduced before, are something of a scoop. Bought by Sean at a car-boot sale, they formerly belonged to GKC's cousin, the Revd John Cecil Frederic Grosjean (1875–1971), who lived for many years in

Reigate and was a perpetual curate, attached to St Mark's Church from 1929.★ Sean has kindly lent them as illustrations for this book; I have also reproduced three of GKC's remarkable drawings. (As with Evelyn Waugh, it was generally thought when he was young that his career would be as an

---

★GKC's mother was Marie Louise Grosjean, before her marriage to Edward Chesterton in 1874. Jeanneret Pierre Frederick Grosjean (the first name is variously spelt, and sometimes appears third in the order of his forenames), was born in Bridport, Dorset, about 1806, apparently of Swiss extraction. He settled in London, where he became a successful 'merchant tailor' with premises in Regent Street. This advertisement for his 'celebrated trowsers' appeared in *Notes and Queries*, 22 April 1854:

CHUBB & SON, 57. St. Paul's Churchyard, London; 28. Lord Street, Liverpool; 16. Market Street, Manchester; and Horseley Fields, Wolverhampton.

guineas. Cases, 12. Cases, 8, 6 Chronom guineas. 50 guineas skilfully guarantee mometer

GROSJEAN'S
CELEBRATED TROWSERS,
16s. per Pair.
109. REGENT STREET.

BENN! Maker to Ordnance

Printed by Thomas Clark Shaw, of No. 10. Stonefield Stree St. Bride, in the City of London; and published by Geor City of London, Publisher, at No. 186. Fleet Street afores

He married Elizabeth Keith in 1831 and died in 1877. They had seven children – Marie Louise was the fifth – but only one son: John Joseph Beaumont Jeanneret Grosjean, a graduate of Lincoln College, Oxford, and a respected analytical chemist, who died young. JJBJG (1843–82) married Una Augusta Wilks (1838–84) in 1870 and had one daughter, Isa Nora (1874–1964) and one son, John Cecil Frederic Grosjean – the Reigate priest. Orphaned at the ages of ten and nine respectively, they were brought up by a relative in Ramsgate, and both lived into advanced old age. Neither married.

Sean Hawkins writes: 'Arthur Cole, who started the Ancient House Bookshop in 1931, was a great friend of the Revd Mr Grosjean – I believe that they lodged in the same gaunt and dreary house on the west side of London Road, leading up to Reigate Hill. Tom Langdon, who took over the bookshop from Arthur Cole in 1947, remembered Grosjean well, and he and other staff at the shop knew him familiarly – among themselves – as "Father Brown".'

artist.) In addition I have used some of Harry Furniss's caricatures of eminent Victorians Chesterton wrote about: that of Charles Dickens is reproduced below.

Illustration 2: Caricature of Charles Dickens by Harry Furniss.

Chesterton was one of the Big Four of Edwardian literature: Belloc, Chesterton, Wells, Shaw. (A wag pointed out that the initial letters of their surnames supplied all the consonants in the punning answer to the question, 'Why is a bee like a rook?' – 'Bee CaWS'.) Wells was indifferent as a public speaker – as

Garrick wrote of Oliver Goldsmith, he 'wrote like an angel, but talk'd like poor Poll'. But the other three – sometimes referred to as the Three Musketeers – were great debaters. Belloc's sparring with F. E. Smith at the Oxford Union was legendary; and Shaw and Chesterton teased each other in public debates. Very often, in print, GKC seems to be debating with an imaginary adversary, setting up a proposition in order to demolish it. The four men frequently disagreed with each other, but remained on friendly terms. Belloc famously defended Chesterton from an academic's sneers –

> Remote and ineffectual don
> That dared attack my Chesterton . . .

Less famous is the ballade he wrote about his admiration for his friend's writings:

I

> I like to read myself to sleep in Bed
> A thing that every honest man has done
> At one time or another, it is said,
> But not as something in the usual run;
> How *I* from ten years old to forty-one
> Have never missed a night; and what I need
> To buck me up is Gilbert Chesterton
> (The only man I regularly read)

II

> *The Illustrated London News* is wed
> To letterpress as stodgy as a bun
> The *Daily News* might just as well be dead
> The *Idler* has a deadly kind of fun
> *The Speaker* is a sort of Sally Lunn
> *The World* is like a small unpleasant weed
> *I take them all because of Chesterton*
> (The only man I regularly read)

III

The memoirs of the Duke of Beachy Head
The memoirs of Lord Hildebrand (his son)
Are things I could have written in my head
So are the memoirs of the Comte de Meun
And as for novels written by the ten,
I'd leave the bloody lot! I know the Breed!
To get us back to Gilbert Chesterton
(The only man I regularly read)

ENVOI

Prince, have you read a book called
'Thoughts upon The Ethos of the Athanasian Creed'?
No matter – it is not by Chesterton
(The only man I regularly read).

Chesterton had strong views on virtually everything. That is the prime requisite in a columnist: it's no use having pappy, tentative, 'either . . . or' views. Think of the best columnists who succeeded GKC – Cassandra (Sir William Connor) of the *Daily Mirror*, Bernard Levin, Keith Waterhouse, Katharine Whitehorn, Alan Coren: writers of pungent, pontifical opinions.

I should make it clear that I do not share all GKC's views. For a start, he was a Roman Catholic and I am not. When I was young I began writing a biography of the Jesuit priest/poet Gerard Manley Hopkins. (Sadly, money ran out and I was unable to complete it.) At a dinner party, a curator from the Victoria & Albert Museum, who was a Roman Catholic, said to me with real anger: 'How dare you, a non-Catholic, write about Gerard Hopkins?' I replied: 'If I were writing about Matthew Hopkins, the Witch-Finder General of the seventeenth century, would I need to believe in witches?' I would claim that my not sharing GKC's faith gives me greater objectivity than if I were his co-religionist; but, under the subject-heading 'Religion' (after 'Literature', it is the largest non-miscellaneous section in the book), I have been careful to give ample representation of his religious views.

Many of his other opinions run counter to what I think; but they have *made* me think. I have included some of the most contentious – indeed, some of the most outrageous and bizarre. They are grenades to explode complacency and 'received opinion' – the opposite of the platitudes and clichés that he despised. I had it in mind to write something like this: 'It is not my rôle to censor GKC; it is my rôle to let him speak for himself.' But that would be not only sanctimonious, but disingenuous. By the very act of selection, I am constantly censoring him. Every anthologist is a censor of sorts – a kind of Micawber in reverse gear, always looking for something to turn down. I do not mean that I have cut out everything I disagreed with: as already indicated, I strongly disagree with many of the views expressed. But my general principle has been: if it is not wise, it should be witty; if it is not witty, it should be wise. Often, of course, it is both.

I have divided the gobbets into sections, with subject-headings and inevitably a large 'Miscellaneous' group. His books on Dickens, Browning, Robert Louis Stevenson and George Bernard Shaw all yielded enough gobbets to have furnished individual sections under their names; but in his study of William Cobbett I found only the rare Cobbett-gobbet that I wanted to include. Because of space considerations it seemed best to absorb all the 'author' quotations into other sections, along with those from GKC's monographs on St Francis and St Thomas Aquinas, most of which naturally belong in the 'Religion' category. My confident hope is that it will be possible to find room for some omitted quotations in a sequel to the present book – *More Wit and Wisdom of G. K. Chesterton.*

Chesterton was proud to call himself a journalist – to acknowledge that he practised the same trade as Daniel Defoe, Dr Johnson and Charles Dickens. I am a journalist too; and I think GKC would approve my having given each gobbet an individual heading. An incorrigible punster himself, he would also, I think, be indulgent to some of the word-play in the headings. However, I have tried to keep this *diablérie* within bounds. It was always rumoured of the macabre cartoonist Charles Addams that from time to time he would turn up at the offices of the *New Yorker* with the same completely unusable cartoon: a naked baby lies on the counter of a delicatessen and a customer is being asked: 'Will you take it wrapped, or eat it here?' After each of these bouts, Addams needed to spend a little time in an asylum. I think I just get away with 'CALVIN DECLINE' for a GKC gobbet (Addams-like, I nearly wrote 'gibbet') about the death of Puritanism in Scotland. But I felt that the padded cell yawned when there swam into my brain this heading for a quotation about the martyrdom of St Thomas of Canterbury – 'THERE'S A HOLE IN MY BECKET'. I changed it to the precedented and inoffensive 'MURDER IN THE CATHEDRAL'.

I have made one large exception to including the views of GKC with which I disagree. He was fiercely and notoriously anti-Semitic. In his columns he is for ever expressing anti-Semitic views; the Jewish characters in his novels and short stories are invariably unappealing to the point of grotesqueness. Reginald Arkell dwelt on this trait in the poem 'G.K.C.' in his book of 1928, *Meet These People*:

> He will not take a glass with you
> Unless your name is Brown.
> For Gilbert oft discloses,
> As only Gilbert can,
> His curious hate for noses,
> Worn by the sons of Moses,
> He'd like them, one supposes,
> Built on a different plan
> But what nobody knows, is
> How first the feud began.

The answer to that question is still unknown. People to whom I've mentioned Chesterton's anti-Semitism say things like:

'Well, it was the common attitude of the time: look at what T. S. Eliot wrote.' But the virulence of Chesterton's racism goes far beyond that endemic attitude. It is impossible to account for its venom. Was he bullied at St Paul's School by a Jewish fellow-pupil? The evidence seems to be that he had Jewish friends there. Did the attitude stem from the extremist Roman Catholic view that the Jews should be reviled because they had killed Christ (a view that rather fails to take account of the fact that Christ was a Jew)? Or did he adopt wholesale the anti-Semitism of his friend and hero Belloc, who persisted in believing Dreyfus guilty long after he was proved innocent? Naturally, I have not chosen any anti-Semitic quotation for this book; but I felt I could not burke mentioning this deplorable aspect of his 'mindset'. While in no way excusing it, a metaphor occurs to me in addressing it. In Japan, by common consent, the most delicious, exquisitely flavoured dish is *fugu* fish. However, before that dish can be enjoyed, a foully poisoned section has to be excised by an expert. Chesterton is a literary *fugu*; and I have cut out the poison. Unlike Winston Churchill and Somerset Maugham – both born in the same year as he – Chesterton did not live to see, with the exposure of Auschwitz and Bergen-Belsen, the horrors that anti-Semitism could lead to. What can be said in his favour is that he was writing stridently anti-Hitler articles as early as 1932.

Another subject on which I have included no gobbets is his campaign (conducted with Hilaire Belloc) for 'Distributism'. I have omitted them on two grounds: first, that Chesterton is uncharacteristically boring whenever he clambers on to this hobby-horse; and second, that the idea of redistributing property so that everybody would have a patch of land, like medieval peasants, was never workable. In 1946 George Orwell wrote to the Revd Henry Rogers: 'Even in Chesterton's lifetime, it was perfectly obvious that this was a hopeless programme in the sense that no large number of people effectively wanted it, and after his death the movement which he had tried to found disintegrated.' (Orwell was rather biting the hand that had fed him, as his first professional work had appeared in Chesterton's magazine *GK's Weekly* in 1928.) Orwell had been still more scathing about the Distributist scheme in his *Road to Wigan Pier* Diary of 1936:

> Liverpool is practically governed by Roman Catholics, The Roman Catholic ideal, at any rate as put forward by the Chesterton-Beach-comber* type of writer, is always in favour of private ownership and against Socialist legislation and 'progress' generally. The Chesterton type of writer wants to see a free peasantry or other small-owner living in his own privately owned and probably insanitary cottage; not a wage-slave living in an excellently appointed Corporation flat and tied down by restrictions as to sanitation etc.

It is only fair to let Chesterton – once and once only – explain what he meant by Distributism. This is what he wrote in *GK's Weekly* on 11 February 1928:

> Distributism . . . really consists of two propositions, one purely economic and the other ethical or psychological . . . The first is that any sort of economic power, whether in cash or credit or the materials that make true wealth, had much better be distributed rather than left undisturbed in the hands of individual millionaires. The second is that the distribution of mere cash or credit is but a mere symbol, or a minor application, of a much more vital principle; that what should be distributed is not merely the legal power of a man over money, but the divine or mystical power of a man over matter . . . It is as easy to see that this ideal is difficult as to see that it is desirable.

The one time Distributism afforded some mild entertainment was when Noël Coward adapted its slogan, 'Two acres and a cow', describing his enemies, Osbert, Sacheverell and Edith Sitwell, as 'two wiseacres and a cow'.

---

* The 'Beachcomber' column in the *Daily Express* was started in 1923 by J. B. Morton (1893–1979), who was, like GKC, a Roman Catholic.

I have also given no space to Chesterton's insufferable anti-Suffragette views, so self-contradictory in a man who fancied himself a defender of individual liberty. (As women have to live under laws voted by Parliament, why could he not see that it is only fair for women to vote MPs into office?) However, I will sneak in here one of his jibes which even some of the leading Suffragettes thought funny: 'Women everywhere declared: "We will not be dictated to!" – and then with one accord became stenographers.'

Chesterton's Distributism had something in common with Mahatma Gandhi's cottage-industry scheme of peasants with their own spinning-wheels; and in fact Chesterton had a surprising and very significant influence on Gandhi. In his recent book *Gandhi: Naked Ambition* (2010), Jad Adams notes that GKC's 'reflections that Indian nationalism was not very Indian if it merely hankered after Western institutions' made a considerable impression on the Indian leader. In January 1910 Gandhi contributed an article to *Indian Opinion*:

> Mr G. K. Chesterton [he wrote] is one of the great writers here. He is an Englishman of a liberal temper. Such is the perfection of his style that his writings are read by millions with great avidity. To *The Illustrated London News* of September 18 [1909] he has contributed an article on Indian awakening, which is worth studying. I too believe that what he has said is reasonable.

Gandhi then proceeded to quote a large chunk of Chesterton's article – in Gujerati. What GKC wrote in the original piece included the following:

> When young Indians talk of independence for India, I get a feeling that they do not understand what they are talking about. I admit that they who demand *swarajya* are fine fellows; most young idealists are fine fellows. I do not doubt that many of the officials are stupid and oppressive. Most of such officials are stupid and oppressive. But when I see the actual papers and know the views of Indian nationalists, I get

bored and feel dubious about them. What they want is not very Indian and not very national. They talk about Herbert Spencer's philosophy and other similar matters. What is the good of the Indian national spirit if they cannot protect themselves from Herbert Spencer? . . .

There is a great difference between a people asking for its own ancient life and a people asking for things that have been wholly invented by somebody else. There is a difference between a conquered people demanding its own institutions and the same people demanding the institutions of the conqueror.

Chesterton added that he would understand it if an Indian said, 'I wish India had always been free from white men and all their works. Everything has its own faults and we prefer our own . . . If you do not like our way of living, we never asked you to. Go, and leave us with it.' What he did not understand was when Indians clamoured for the judge's wig, the Budget, to be prime minister or edit the *Daily Mail*. Those were western attributes and institutions: we invented them and therefore 'have some of the authority that belongs to founders'. It was, GKC thought, 'as if I were to go into Tibet and demand of the Lama that I should be treated as a Mahatma'. In conclusion, he wrote that he was not opposing Indian nationalism; his difficulty was that 'the Indian nationalist is not national'.

Having quoted the passage, Gandhi commented:

Indians must reflect over these views of Mr Chesterton and consider what they should rightly demand. What is the way to make the Indian people happy? May it not be that we seek to advance our own interests in the name of the Indian people? Or, that we have been endeavouring to destroy what the Indian people have carefully nurtured through thousands of years? I, for one, was led by Mr Chesterton's article to all these reflections . . .

It is not, therefore, an exaggeration to claim that GKC's words affected the Indian independence movement. The influence that a writer has is some gauge of his effectiveness. Judged by that standard, Chesterton is seen to have been surpassingly – one might say pre-eminently – effective, in a way that Cassandra, Bernard Levin, Keith Waterhouse, Katharine Whitehorn and Alan Coren, with all their varied merits, have not been.

He influenced George Orwell in a negative way by setting his futurist novel, *The Napoleon of Notting Hill*, in the year 1984. It has been plausibly argued that Orwell gave the title *Nineteen Eighty-Four* to his futurist novel to rebuke GKC for his optimistic predictions. But Bernard Crick has suggested a more central way in which GKC influenced Orwell's novel. When Winston dreams that he has walked through a pitch-dark room and heard a voice say, 'We shall meet in the place where there is no darkness', the relationship of light and dark had its source in the final chapter of GKC's *The Man Who Was Thursday* – which it is known Orwell had read.

Orwell wrote in 1946 that GKC's Distributist doctrines reappear essentially unchanged in T. S. Eliot's idea of a Christian society. That is not surprising: T. S. Eliot is one of the most assiduous plagiarists in the whole of English literature – he stole the title of *The Waste Land*, and much besides, from a minor Kentucky poet called Madison Cawein.

If you ask who are now the two greatest cult figures in English literature of the twentieth century – particularly in America – the answers are J. R. R. Tolkien and C. S. Lewis. Both writers were greatly influenced by Chesterton. In 2007 Alison Milbank published *Chesterton and Tolkien as Theologians*, a book whose stated aim was 'to demonstrate that . . . G. K. Chesterton was an important influence both on Tolkien's fiction and his literary criticism of the fairy tale'. In the first part of the book she offered a literary reading of Tolkien's writing through what she discerned to be his 'specifically Chestertonian poetics'. In the second part she argued that it is 'through these same stylistic tropes that an implicitly Tolkienesque theology of art emerges: literature is shown to perform theology'.

As a university teacher, Milbank had found it hard to identify a contemporary intellectual or theoretical context in which to situate Tolkien's fiction. Others had done good work on his Anglo-Saxon sources and his membership of the Inklings group, but there was a dearth of straightforward literary analysis of his way of writing. What contemporary writers had Tolkien read outside his professional work? Examining his published letters and essays, Milbank was struck by the frequency with which he referred quite casually to the earlier writer of fantastic fiction. In one letter he quoted GKC's characteristic remark that 'anything that is announced as "here to stay" is bound shortly to be replaced'. In 1944 he mentioned that his young daughter – no doubt at parental suggestion – was reading GKC's 'The Ballad of the White Horse'. Milbank writes:

> Reading 'The Ballad of the White Horse' after *The Lord of the Rings* is to recognize a great affinity and a common project. Despite the anachronism of Chesterton's ballad form for an Anglo-Saxon voice, the whole spirit of King Alfred's position on the cusp between paganism and Christianity is true to Tolkien's understanding of *Beowulf* as a poem that is a careful preservation by a Christian of pagan tradition. Alfred has the White Horse of the Oxfordshire vale recut, 'Because it is only Christian men/Guard even heathen things', just as Tolkien argues that it is Christianity that preserves the pagan in his essay, 'Beowulf: the Monsters and the Critics'.

Milbank observes that it is in Tolkien's essay 'On Fairy Stories' 'that Chesterton is cited most carefully and specifically'. In the essay Tolkien supports Chesterton's idea of children's sense of justice against Andrew Lang's tendency to soften some of the material he adapted in his Fairy Books. In the rest of her book, Milbank draws convincing analogies between Chesterton and Tolkien in their deployment of fantasy, the grotesque, paradox and riddles. In her Conclusion, however, she makes a distinction between them:

Chesterton and Tolkien offer us different ways to achieve joyous apprehension of otherness. The earlier writer always takes us back to the diurnal world to see it with new eyes, and this will be the beginning of our reconciliation with nature, if we are to live peaceably and without further harm to the earth and its atmosphere. Tolkien . . . always takes us further along towards the transcendent.

As we have seen, Evelyn Waugh used a quotation from Chesterton as a heading in *Brideshead Revisited*. Trevor Huddleston took a phrase from 'The Ballad of the White Horse' as the title of his 1956 book *Naught for Your Comfort*. A writer of roughly their generation who was less captivated by GKC was the subject of my last book, John Betjeman. In the early 1960s the BBC producer Kenneth Savidge made a series of television films with Betjeman entitled *ABC of Churches*. 'B' was inevitably Blisland, Cornwall, one of Betjeman's favourite churches. 'X', through a brainwave of the poet, was St Cross, Winchester, the chapel of the almshouse where I now live: the crew were given sherry by the disreputable Brother Dick Young, the original of 'Captain Grimes' in Evelyn Waugh's *Decline and Fall*. 'U' had to be Uffington, where Betjeman and his wife had spent their early married life. That film began with Betjeman bowing three times into the eye of the White Horse above the village. Savidge wanted him to recite Chesterton's lines:

> Before the gods that made the gods
> Had seen their sunrise pass
> The White Horse of the White Horse Vale
> Was cut out of the grass.

Usually Betjeman did whatever Savidge asked him to do; but he absolutely refused to recite Chesterton's verse. Why? In the biography, I hazarded two possible reasons: first, that maybe Betjeman was jealous (*he* was the poet of Uffington) or second, that he felt distaste for GKC's Roman Catholicism, the religion to which his wife's defection had helped to break up their marriage. But now I think there may have been a reason more powerful than either of those two. When the Uffington film was made, fewer than ten years had elapsed since 1955, when *Surprised by Joy* was published, the early memoirs of Betjeman's former tutor and *bête noire*, C. S. Lewis. Betjeman would certainly have read that book; and in it he would have found his arch-enemy lavishing the highest praise on Chesterton. That, for Betjeman, could well have been enough to settle Chesterton's hash. Lewis had written:

> It was here [in the wartime army] that I first read a volume of Chesterton's essays. I had never heard of him and had no idea of what he stood for; nor can I quite understand why he made such an immediate conquest of me. It might have been expected that my pessimism, my atheism, and my hatred of sentiment would have made him to me the least congenial of all authors. It would almost seem that Providence, or some 'second cause' of a very obscure kind, quite over-rules our previous tastes when it decides to bring two minds together. Liking an author may be as involuntary and improbable as falling in love. I was by now a sufficiently experienced reader to distinguish liking from agreement. I did not need to accept what Chesterton said in order to enjoy it. His humour was of the kind which I like best – not 'jokes' imbedded in the page like currants in a cake, still less (what I cannot endure), a general tone of flippancy and jocularity, but the humour which is not in any way separable from the argument but is rather (as Aristotle would say) the 'bloom' on dialectic itself. The sword glitters not because the swordsman set out to make it glitter but because he is fighting for his life and therefore moving it very quickly. For the critics who think Chesterton frivolous or 'paradoxical' I have to work hard to feel even pity; sympathy is out of the question. Moreover, strange as it may seem, I liked him for his goodness.

Was ever a tribute from one great writer to another more heartfelt, more finely expressed or more just? Lewis added:

> In reading Chesterton . . . I did not know what I was letting myself in for. A young man who wishes to remain a sound Atheist cannot be

too careful of his reading. There are traps everywhere – 'Bibles laid open, millions of surprises', as Herbert says, 'fine nets and stratagems'. God is, if I may say it, very unscrupulous.

Still an atheist when he first read Chesterton, Lewis began to think that 'Chesterton had more sense than all the other moderns put together; bating, of course, his Christianity.' Then he read GKC's *The Everlasting Man* 'and for the first time saw the whole Christian outline of history set out in a form that seemed to me to make sense'.

> Somehow I contrived not to be too badly shaken. You will remember that I already thought Chesterton the most sensible man alive 'apart from his Christianity'. Now, I verily believe, I thought – I didn't of course *say*; words would have revealed the nonsense – that Christianity itself was very sensible 'apart from its Christianity'.

There is no doubt that Chesterton had a large responsibility for transforming Lewis into what he became – the most famous proselytizing Christian layman since GKC himself. (By an irony, Betjeman would be Lewis's nearest rival for that title, but the man who was Summoned by Bells was never reconciled to the man who was Surprised by Joy.)

It is often alleged that a great religion has nothing to fear from criticism. The same might be said of a great writer; so I do not scruple to quote the most malignant attack ever made on Chesterton. Like most attacks, it has a glimmer of truth in it. For a time – by one of those weird quirks of history, like the ones that ensured that Cézanne would be at school with Zola, and John Piper with Graham Sutherland; that T. S. Eliot would teach John Betjeman at Highgate Junior School; and that Harper Lee would be a childhood playmate of Truman Capote in Alabama (*To Kill a Mockingbird in Cold Blood*, as it were) – the Irish playwright Sean O'Casey lived at 49 Overstrand Mansions in Battersea, next door to No. 48 where the Chestertons had lived. In his final volume of memoirs, *Sunset and Evening Star*,

O'Casey scorned Maisie Ward's statement, in her biography of GKC, that he visited Battersea pubs to discuss local politics with local people. He lammed into Chesterton:

> These visits – if they ever occurred – were evidently part of those tip, touch, habits which coloured his whole life. Rushing round, he tipped Shaw, Dickens, Browning, John of Austria, breathless with running all the time; and as he ran past life, he shouted gee gee up to the white horse, dismounting for a while to chuck the roman catholic church under the chin. There's the brave horseman, there's his two min; there he goes out and here he goes in; chin chucky chin chucky under the chin. He never waited a second to sit down in any room of thought, contenting himself with peeping round the door, throwing in a coloured puff-ball of braggart doctrinal remark that went round the room of life till it fell into dull dust when some curious finger chanced to touch it.

When Henry James's novels are filmed or televised, it is possible to cut out a great deal of his verbiage and tortured circumlocution, leaving crisp dialogue. In anthologizing Chesterton, something similar can happen. In his book of 1969, *The Rise and Fall of the Man of Letters*, John Gross (magnanimously, considering that he is Jewish) paid handsome tribute to GKC, but qualified his praise: there was dross with the gold.

> He was a man of remarkable gifts, far more remarkable than his present overclouded reputation would suggest. At his finest, for instance, he was a wittier writer than Oscar Wilde or Max Beerbohm (as Beerbohm himself readily acknowledged): wittier because he had a deeper understanding of life. But as he turns the barrel-organ, and the paradoxes come thumping out, the wit can easily pall and the profundity can get completely overlooked. The best is so very good, the worst is so flashy and cheap.

Clearly, then, the GKC anthologist needs the discrimination to winnow. I will not disguise that some of the gobbets have been winkled out of a morass of blather, rant and guff. What do we find in the 'good' Chesterton, as against the 'flashy and cheap' GKC? Dazzling artistry with words, usually under-pinned by a stringent morality – what C. S. Lewis meant when he used the word 'goodness' – which in turn is reinforced by GKC's faith. (I except the times when he is just frolicking and being engagingly silly, as when he says, of jelly:★ 'I don't like a pudding that's afraid of me.')

Pace John Gross, Chesterton's deployment of paradox is one of his great strengths. (I admit it can become wearisome when he overdoes it, especially in his later writings.) Though Chesterton loathed and rebelled against the *fin de siècle* 'deca-dence' of the 1890s, he did learn the trick of paradox from Wilde. In *The Man Who Was Thursday*, a young woman asks the central character, Syme: 'Do the people who talk like you and my brother often mean what they say? Do you mean what you say now?' GKC's habit of standing propositions on their head caused many to ask those kinds of question. To another character in the novel, Syme gives this answer: 'You thought a paradox might wake men up to a neglected truth.' In other words, a paradox is not to be taken literally: it is a catalyst. Chesterton's other great weapon is his use of analogy – what Belloc called his 'parallelism'. Whenever he writes: 'You might as well say that . . .' (a phrase straight out of *Alice in Wonderland*), you know that some devastating *reductio ad absurdum* is on the way. Chesterton is a supreme wordsmith; but he is never just making verbal patterns – that would be the 'art for art's sake' that he deplored in the Wildean aesthetes. As the insistently cerebral C. S. Lewis perceived, even GKC's jokes were organic, not mere embellishments.

When Chesterton died in 1936 there was an outpouring of tributes to him by journalists who knew him as one of their own. One of the most affecting was by Robert Lynd, in the *News Chronicle*:

★For American readers: what the British call jelly, you call jello. What you call jelly, we call jam.

The truth is [he wrote], he never ceased to be a poet even when he was writing prose.

He once said that if he were a millionaire he would like to 'chuck his money about' – not to deserving people, but 'just to chuck it about'.

In literature and journalism he may be said to have chucked his genius about. It seems to me likely that we shall still for many generations to come be collecting the gold pieces that he has strewn with such magnificent recklessness.

That is a pretty good job description of the task I have set myself in this book.

BIOGRAPHY

Illustration 3: Gilbert and his brother Cecil, with mother, Marie.
Photo courtesy of Sean Hawkins (see. p. xiii).

Gilbert Keith Chesterton was born on 29 May 1874 in
Sheffield Terrace, Campden Hill, London. His father, Edward,
was the comfortably-off director of the estate agent Chesterton's, which still exists in Kensington. As already mentioned, his

mother, *née* Marie Louise Grosjean, was of a family long resident in England but originally from French Switzerland. A brother, Cecil, was born five years after Gilbert: the two argued incessantly, but were close. A baby sister died when Gilbert was very young.

As a child, Gilbert loved fairy tales and playing with a toy theatre made by Edward, He was absent-minded and untidy. He was educated at Colet Court, then St Paul's School, where after fighting him he became a lifelong friend of Edmund Clerihew Bentley, some of whose 'clerihews' he later illustrated. He was considered a bit of a dunce: that was to give him empathy with St Thomas Aquinas, who was known as 'the Dumb Ox'. Where Gilbert first shone was in the Junior Debating Club, formed at school and continued long afterwards.

Several of his friends won scholarships at Oxford and Cambridge; but Chesterton, whose skill at drawing was already apparent, went first to Philip Hermogenes Calderon's art school in St John's Wood,★ then to the Slade School. He was still skinny, as a self-portrait shows (Illustration 4). At the Slade he went through some kind of Dark Night of the Soul. He became friendly with a man he later called 'The Diabolist', and seems to have dabbled in black magic. One of his friends, finding a notebook full of Chesterton's 'horrible' drawings, asked another: 'Is Chesterton going mad?'

After that (as he eloquently recalled in the dedicatory poem to Bentley which prefaces *The Man Who Was Thursday*) he reacted against 1890s 'decadence'. Walt Whitman and Robert Louis Stevenson seemed to him the antidotes to Pater, Swinburne and Wilde.

While at the Slade he attended English lectures at University College. (The Slade was part of the University of London.)

★Calderon was a member of the group of artists known as 'The St John's Wood Clique', of which the best-known member was W. F. Yeames, who painted *'And When Did You Last See Your Father?'* See B. Hillier, 'The St John's Wood Clique', *Apollo,* May 1964.

Illustration 4: Self-portrait.

There he met a fellow student, Ernest Hodder Williams, of the publishing house Hodder & Stoughton. He gave Chesterton some books on art to review for *The Bookman*, a monthly magazine published by the firm. That was Chesterton's first professional commission. He worked briefly for a publisher called Redway; then, for some years, for Fisher Unwin.

In 1896 he met Frances Blogg, daughter of a diamond merchant who lived in the 'arty' suburb of Bedford Park, where Yeats lived for a time, as recorded in a Chesterton drawing (Illustration 5). Chesterton's mother disapproved of her son's growing friendship with Frances: she had another girl in mind for him. But Chesterton was in love and, after a long engagement, he and Frances were married, in 1901, by the Socialist priest Conrad Noel.

Illustration 5: Drawing by GKC of Bedford Park. The man on the left is
W. B. Yeats. The silhouetted figure is GKC.

During the Boer War, Chesterton, always an anti-Imperialist,
was of the small minority who were 'pro-Boer', an unpopular
stance. In 1899 he began to write for *The Speaker*, a Liberal
weekly edited by J. L. Hammond. There he met Hilaire Belloc:
they became so inseparable that Bernard Shaw invented the
pantomime horse 'the Chesterbelloc'. Chesterton's early biographer Maisie Ward writes of 'the intellectual flame struck out
by one mind against the other'. Belloc made Chesterton more
political and convinced him of the merits of Distributism. He,

too, was a pro-Boer. They were not pacifists. They disliked the war because they thought it would damage England to be fighting for an unjust cause at the bidding of 'alien financiers'.

By the end of 1900 Chesterton was becoming well known. His book of that year, *Greybeards at Play*, contained three satirical poems, one of them entitled 'The Disastrous Spread of Aestheticism in All Classes'. In 1901 his first book of collected essays appeared, *The Defendant*. He became a friend of Max Beerbohm and Bernard Shaw. The 'toby jug' Chesterton of legend was literally taking shape. He was becoming gross. Somebody joked that he had given up his seat on a bus to two women. Shaw prodded him in his vast stomach and asked what he was going to call the baby. 'If it is a boy, I shall call him John,' GKC replied. 'If a girl, Mary. And if it is wind, as I think it probably is, I shall call it George Bernard Shaw.' He wore a voluminous cloak, a broad-brimmed hat and pince-nez. He was an habitué of Fleet Street. Frank Swinnerton recorded a description given him by Charles Masterman of:

> . . . how Chesterton used to sit writing his articles in a Fleet Street café, sampling and mixing a terrible conjunction of drinks, while many waiters hovered about him, partly in awe, and partly in case he should leave the restaurant without paying for what he had had. One day . . . the head waiter approached Masterman. 'Your friend,' he whispered, admiringly, 'he very clever man. He sit and laugh. And then he write. And then he laugh at what he write.'

Comparisons were inevitably made with that other haunter of Fleet Street, Dr Johnson. Chesterton was in demand to play him in pageants (Illustration 6).

He became a Saturday columnist on the *Daily News*, edited by A. G. Gardiner. Gardiner recalled:

> [His copy] arrived in all sorts of shapes and by all sorts of means . . . It was written on any kind of paper that might be at hand, once, at any rate, when GKC was in the throes of moving house, on a piece of

Illustration 6: Chesterton as Dr Johnson.

wallpaper. He was completely negligent about money, and frequently without any; when he arrived at the office with his copy in that condition, the commissionaire would have to pay the taxi fare.

When Gardiner's eldest daughter asked GKC to inscribe a page in her autograph album, he wrote 'Some Recollections of Journalism', of which these are extracts:

> It is as well that you should know
> The truth about that empty show,

> That vast and histrionic ruse,
> Which calls itself 'the *Daily News*'.
> 'Tis a dark truth, if truth be said,
> We tried at every other trade
> And we have found (with joy I sing)
> That we were bad at everything.
> When upon any work our wit
> We tried, we made a mess of it.
> When your Papa, exultant, sailed
> A pirate, he distinctly failed . . .
> One secret more: one person writes
> All the whole paper all the nights.
> He writes on war and war's redress,
> On literature and ladies' dress.
> Upon the commerce of Hong Kong
> He is particularly strong.
> His beard is long, his gestures free
> And his initials GKC.

The *Daily News* was owned by the chocolate-making Cadbury family. GKC's connection with the paper came to a painful end in 1913, after he wrote a poem in contempt of cocoa, which contained these lines:

> Tea, although an Oriental,
> Is a gentleman at least.
> Cocoa is a cad and coward;
> Cocoa is a vulgar beast.
> Cocoa is a crawling, cringing,
> Lying, loathsome swine and clown
> And may very well be grateful
> To the fool that takes him down.

Alongside his journalism the great spate of books continued: *Twelve Types* (1902); *Robert Browning* (1903); *G. F. Watts* and his first novel, *The Napoleon of Notting Hill* (both 1904); and *The Club of Queer Trades* and *Heretics* – both in 1905, the year he began contributing his long-running weekly column to *The Illustrated London News*. *Charles Dickens* followed in 1906, and in 1908 no fewer than three GKC books were published: *The Man Who Was Thursday*, *All Things Considered* and *Orthodoxy*. It was a phenomenal output for a young man.

After a honeymoon on the Norfolk Broads, Chesterton and Frances had first lived in a small house in Edwardes Square, Kensington, lent them by a friend of Frances. After a few months they moved to Overstrand Mansions, Battersea, where the rest of their London life was spent. There were never any children. Chesterton told his brother that Frances had been resistant to sex; but in a malicious book Cecil's widow (he died just after service in the First World War) mentioned that GKC had only reached puberty very late and hinted he was impotent. In 1909 the couple moved to Overroads, Beaconsfield. There were two more books in that year; four in 1911, two in 1912; a book and a play, *Magic*, in 1913

In 1913 Cecil Chesterton appeared in the dock at the Old Bailey, charged with criminal libel. Described as 'spittingly, uncontrollably anti-Semitic', Cecil had alleged in his magazine *The New Witness* that the Attorney-General, Sir Rufus Isaacs, and the Chancellor of the Exchequer, David Lloyd George, had engaged in corrupt financial dealings in the shares of the Marconi Company, which was setting up a radio communications system throughout the British Empire. GKC took his brother's side in the scandal; but Cecil was fined £100 and was lucky not to go to prison.

Four more GKC books appeared in 1914, but in that year he fell seriously ill and was in a coma for three months. It was to answer the many letters of sympathy which flooded in that Frances asked Freda Spencer to come and help. In 1915 Chesterton recovered from his illness, which was a kind of dropsy (Dr Johnson again), and published *Letters to an Old Garibaldian*, *Poems* and *The Crimes of England*. In 1916 he replaced Cecil as editor of *The New Witness* (later renamed *GK's Weekly*). A visit to Ireland in 1919 led to his book *Irish Impressions*, which was published in 1919, in which year he went to Palestine. In 1920 he made a lecture tour of the United States.

In 1922, the year his *Eugenics and Other Evils*, *What I Saw in America* and *The Man Who Knew Too Much* were published, Chesterton was received into the Roman Catholic Church by Father John O'Connor (the part original of the Father Brown character). *Fancies versus Fads* and *St Francis of Assisi* appeared the next year. The procession of books continued. He was deeply involved in Distributism. In 1927 he visited Poland. In 1928 there was a broadcast debate with Bernard Shaw, published as *Do We Agree?* He visited Rome in 1929 and in 1930–31 undertook a second lecture tour of the United States – on the model of his idol, Dickens. An important late book was *Chaucer*, in 1932, the year in which he began to broadcast regularly on the BBC in his squeaky, high-pitched voice.

He died on 14 June 1936. That day, Hilaire Belloc sent a telegram to Frances:

FRANCES CHESTERTON TOP MEADOW BEACONSFIELD
THE NEWS REACHED ME IN SUSSEX LATE GOD BLESS
AND HELP YOU AM HAVING MASSES SEND ME ANY
INSTRUCTIONS ADDRESS BELLOC COOLHAM HILARY

Chesterton's *Autobiography* was published posthumously in 1936.

1

TASTERS

As hors d'oeuvre, here are some of GKC's pithiest and most pungent one- and two-liners.

TILL DEATH DO US PART

Marriage is a duel to the death, which no man of honour should decline.

Manalive, London 1915

THE VIRTUES OF NONSENSE

There is a sort of abstract beauty in the irresponsible inverted wit which we call Nonsense, which has no moral to preach and no abuse to scourge.

The Illustrated London News, 4 July 1931

OPEN WIDE

The cure for a stuffy house is to open the windows, not knock down the walls.

The Illustrated London News, 5 March 1927

'ON READING "GOD"'

Mr Middleton Murry explains that his book with this title records his farewell to God.

> Murry, on finding *le Bon Dieu*
> *Chose difficile à croire,*
> Illogically said 'Adieu',
> But God said: 'Au Revoir'.

Published in *GK's Weekly*, 1932; reprinted in *GK's Miscellany*, London 1934

GIRL GUIDES

AM IN MARKET HARBOROUGH WHERE OUGHT I TO BE
GILBERT

Telegram from GKC to his wife Frances, British Library Add. MSS
73276A

THE POINT OF WAR

War is not the best way of settling differences; it is the only way of preventing their being settled for you.

The Illustrated London News, 24 July 1915

WALKING THE PLANK

If I am made to walk the plank by a pirate, it is vain for me to offer, as a common-sense compromise, to walk along the plank for a reasonable distance. It is exactly about the reasonable distance that the pirate and I differ.

What's Wrong with the World, London 1910

POSTAL STRIKE

A sort of anxiety came back into the priest's eyes – the anxiety of a man who has run against a post in the dark and wonders for a moment whether he has hurt it.

'The Oracle of the Dog' (*The Father Brown Stories*)

GODFORSAKEN

If there were no God, there would be no atheists.

Where All Roads Lead, London 1922

FOLK WISDOM

The innkeeper Humphrey Pump is cooking a fungus in an old frying-pan; and he knows which one to cook.

He was the old-fashioned English naturalist, like Gilbert White or even Izaak Walton, who learnt things not academically like an American Professor, but actually, like an American Indian.

The Flying Inn, London 1914

BANGING ON

On foreign writers of whom we hear nothing until they commit or are the victims of crime.

The pen may be mightier than the sword, but it is not so noisy as the pistol.

The Illustrated London News, 15 December 1923

THE CORN IS RED

Of the Russian revolutionaries.

Their wild oats were far less horrible than their harvest festival.
The thing was much more respectable as a rebellion than it is
as a government.

The Illustrated London News, 12 November 1921

QUOTE, MISQUOTE

It is the most sincere compliment to an author to misquote
him. It means that his work has become a part of our mind and
not merely of our library.

GK's Weekly, 31 December 1927

YOU NEVER CAN'T TELL

Gale said: 'You know how silent boys have been about
incredible abuses in bad schools. Whether or no it's false to say
a girl can't keep a secret, it's often really the ruin of a boy that
he can keep a secret.'

The Poet and the Lunatics, London 1929

THE COLD CALL

. . . The Imperial Pioneer is essentially a commercial traveller;
and a commercial traveller is essentially a person who goes to
see people because they don't want to see him.

'The Sentimentalist', *Alarms and Discursions*, London 1911

RINGING THE CHANGES

Progress should mean that we are always changing the world to fit the vision; instead we are always changing the vision.

Orthodoxy, London 1908

VISA TROUBLE

[The form GKC filled in to get an American visa] was a little like a freer form of the game called 'Confessions' which my friends and I invented in our youth; an examination paper containing questions like, 'If you saw a rhinoceros in the front garden, what would you do?' One of my friends, I remember, wrote: 'Take the pledge.'

What I saw in America, London 1922

PAX VOBISCUM

It takes three to make a quarrel. There is needed a peace-maker.

The Thing, New York 1930

NIHIL OBSTAT

[Men of the 1890s] were rather nihilists than atheists; for there is a difference between worshipping Nothing and not worshipping anything.

Robert Louis Stevenson, London 1907

WINTRY SMILE

GKC suggests that one of the pleasurable aspects of Christmas is that it occurs in the winter.

All comfort must be based on discomfort. Man chooses when he wishes to be most joyful the very moment when the whole material universe is most sad.

Introduction to Dickens's *Christmas Books*, London 1907

DIGNITY MAINTAINED

No lady in Henry James ever skipped.*

Robert Louis Stevenson, London 1907

*But some of his readers did. – BH

BRAIN DRAIN

I am sure that in so far as there is any sort of social breakdown, it is not so much a moral breakdown as a mental breakdown. It is much more like a softening of the brain than a hardening of the heart.

The Illustrated London News, 13 March 1926

THE ENGLISH SATIRIST

GKC is reviewing the humorous columns, in book form, of 'Beachcomber'.

It is difficult to define what being English means [in satire]. It is not exactly that his bark is worse than his bite, for his bite is sometimes very formidable. But it is that he actually enjoys barking more than he enjoys biting.

The Illustrated London News, 4 July 1931

BY JOVE!

It is by no means so very certain that a Roman believed in Jupiter as it is that a Catholic believes in Jesus Christ or a Mahometan in Mahomet.

The Illustrated London News, 28 January 1928

HIDDEN DEPTHS

The Englishman is the one man really made for psychoanalysis. He really does instinctively erect screens and scenery, half symbolic and half secretive, to protect a hidden thought.

GK's Weekly, 23 January 1936

THE PLOT THINS

I have seen a number of detective stories in which the same writer first failed to mystify and then failed to elucidate.

The Illustrated London News, 23 January 1926

COMMUNISM AT THE ALTAR

'With all my worldly goods I thee endow' is the only satisfactory Bolshevik proclamation that has ever been made about property.

'On Dependence and Independence', *All I Survey*, London 1933

JONATHAN SWIFT

I fear he was largely saved from scepticism by a contempt for
the sceptics.

'On Jonathan Swift', *All I Survey*, London 1933

THE CAMERA *CAN* LIE

An honest man cannot mislead in watercolour. His soul is
purified by passing through all the colours of a child's paint-
box. The real thing for misleading is photography.

The Illustrated London News, 7 June 1913

TRAVELLER'S JOY

The most valuable book we can read, about countries we have
visited, is that which recalls to us something that we did
notice, but did not notice that we noticed.

The Illustrated London News, 2 February 1924

TAKE A BREAK

The only people who ought to be allowed to work are the
people who are able to shirk.

Introduction to *Little Dorrit*, London 1908

DEFECTIVE STORY

Bad men are almost without exception conceited, but they
are commonly conceited of their defects.

Robert Browning, London 1903

SHALL I COMPARE THEE . . . ?

Progress is a comparative of what we have not settled the superlative.

Heretics, London 1905

PAST IMPERFECT

The past is not what it was.

A Short History of England, London 1917

PLAYING TO THE GALLERY

I do feel a certain contempt for those who . . . charge a man with talking for effect, as if there were anything else to talk for.

Robert Louis Stevenson, London 1907

FREE VERSE

Vers libre, or nine-tenths of it, is not a new metre any more than sleeping in a ditch is a new school of architecture.

Fancies versus Fads, London 1923

A PROPHECY

Herr Hitler is undoubtedly ready to wage another Great War to make the world safe from Democracy.

The Illustrated London News, 3 December 1932

ANOTHER PROPHECY

Those who ask us what we shall do with the docks seldom seem to ask themselves what the docks will do with themselves, if our commerce steadily declines like that of so many commercial cities in the past.

The Outline of Sanity, London 1926

TROUBLE IN STORE

. . . If I wrote a romance about the future (which Heaven avert!), I should describe a state in which the big shops and businesses had become almost independent kingdoms or clans, the power of the employer over clerks and shopmen enormous; the power of the State over the employer comparatively slight.

The Illustrated London News, 16 December 1911

DOGMA

'Yes,' said Father Brown. 'I always like a dog, so long as he isn't spelt backwards.'

'The Oracle of the Dog' (*The Father Brown Stories*)

TIME TO KILL

Heresies die faster than they can be killed.

GK's Weekly, 19 June 1926

LOATHSOME

GKC is criticizing Stevenson's The Ebb Tide.

I do not object to the author creating such a loathsome person as Mr Attwater; but I do rather object to his creating him and not loathing him.

Robert Louis Stevenson, London 1907

DICKENS'S STATURE

Critics have called Keats and others who died young 'the great Might-have-beens of literary history' . . . Dickens . . . was a great Was.

Introduction to Dickens's *Christmas Stories*, London 1910

GENIUSES CLASH

Men do not like another man because he is a genius, least of all when they happen to be geniuses themselves.

Robert Browning, London 1903

THE BATTLEGROUND OF SURREY

Surrey is the debatable land between London and England. It is not a county, but a border; it is there that South London meets and makes war on Sussex.

The Illustrated London News, 9 July 1910

BONE IDOL

William Cobbett brought back the bones of his hero Tom Paine from America to England.

I wonder what he said when asked if he had anything to declare?

William Cobbett, London 1925

THAT PLAYS THE KING

I think Claudius [in *Hamlet*] is a very fine and true study of the Usurper; because he is the man who really wants to be King. A man must take the monarchy very seriously to be a Usurper.

The Illustrated London News, 12 September 1925

AWAY WITH THE FAIRIES

The fairy tale discusses what a sane man will do in a mad world.

Orthodoxy, London 1909

BY HIS OWN HAND

The suicide . . . defiles every flower by refusing to live for its sake.

Orthodoxy, London 1909

A LITTLE OF WHAT YOU FANCY

When giving treats to friends or children, give them what they like, emphatically not what is good for them.

Chesterton Review, February 1984

MOB RULE

A real mob is sadly rare in modern politics.

The Illustrated London News, 26 September 1925

DECLINE AND RISE

Gibbon is now a classic; that is, he is quoted instead of being read.

The Illustrated London News, 5 June 1926

INFIRMITY OF PURPOSE

When everything about a people is for the time growing weak and ineffective, it begins to talk about efficiency. So it is when a man's body is a wreck he begins, for the first time, to talk about health. Vigorous organisms talk not about their processes, but about their aims.

Heretics, London 1906

DEVOUT AGNOSTICS

[In the mid–Victorian period] Men were . . . agnostics: they said, 'We do not know'; but not one of them ever ventured to say, 'We do not care.'

G. F. Watts, London 1904

A TURN FOR THE WORSE

I have not the slightest difficulty in imagining the world of the future taking a turn which would bring back the fact, if not the form, of witch-hunting and slavery and the persecution of heresies.

The Illustrated London News, 9 June 1934

QUIETLY ENCOURAGING

Father Brown had a talent for being silent in an encouraging way.

'The Curse of the Golden Cross' (*The Father Brown Stories*)

MYSTAGOGUES

'He's a mystagogue,' said Father Brown, with innocent promptitude. 'There are quite a lot of them about; the sort of men about town who hint to you in Paris cafés and cabarets that they've lifted the veil of Isis or know the secret of Stonehenge. . .'

'The Arrow of Heaven' (*The Father Brown Stories*)

NIGHTMARES CAN BE FUN

There is nothing so delightful as a nightmare – when you know it is a nightmare.

'The Nightmare', *Alarms and Discursions*, London 1911

. . . AND INWARDLY DIGEST

Nobody, strictly speaking, is happier on account of his digestion. He is happy because he is so constituted as to forget all about it . . . There is about digestion this peculiarity throwing a great light on human pessimism, that it is one of the many things which we never speak of as existing until they go wrong.

Robert Browning, London 1903

THROWAWAY LINES

GKC suggests that Dickens's genius appears in the 'broken outbreaks' of his journalism.

If a man has flung away bad ideas he has shown his sense, but if he has flung away good ideas he has shown his genius.

Introduction to Dickens's *Christmas Stories*, London 1910

BREAKING UP WITH THE JONESES

The Bible tells us to love our neighbours, and also to love our enemies; probably because they are generally the same people.

The Illustrated London News, 2 July 1910

ZEAL FOR CHANGE

The reformer is always right about what is wrong. He is generally wrong about what is right.

The Illustrated London News, 28 October 1922

'ON A PROHIBITIONIST POEM'

The second stanza of a two-stanza poem.

> . . . Though wine that seeks the loftiest habitation
> Went to the heads of Villon and Verlaine,
> Yet Hiram Hopper needs no inspiration
> But water on the brain.

The Collected Poems of G. K. Chesterton, London 1933

SOARING AMBITION

On Sir Arthur Travers, barrister.

He's one of those men who are ambitious even when they've satisfied their ambition.

'The Mirror of the Magistrate' (*The Father Brown Stories*)

IF YOU CAN'T, PRAISE

It is possibly the difference between D'Annunzio and Nietzsche, both national and personal, that Nietzsche praised fighting and D'Annunzio fought.

The Illustrated London News, 7 October 1922

BROKEN VOWELS

There is what is always described rather curiously as 'broken English', and it is obviously necessary to be a foreigner in order to bring one's broken English to perfection.

The Illustrated London News, 12 December 1931

MUTE INGLORIOUS MICHELANGELOS?

I find it hard to convince myself that Michael Angelo is no longer to be seen because a vast mob of Michael Angelos are struggling in the street.

The Illustrated London News, 24 January 1925

MOTE AND BEAM

The Press is shocked at corruption in the police – as if there were no corruption in the Press.

The Illustrated London News, 11 February 1928

HEIR APERIENT

On birth control.

I have always used the parallel of the man who took emetics in order to eat six dinners a day.

GK's Weekly, 25 April 1935

THE RIVALS

I do not . . . believe that Humanism and Religion are rivals on equal terms. I believe it is a rivalry between the pools and the fountain; or between the firebrands and the fire.

The Thing, New York 1930

AS BIG AS THE RITZ?

When I first went into one of the big New York hotels, the first impression was certainly its bigness. It was called the Biltmore; and I wondered how many national humorists had made the obvious comment of wishing they had built less.

What I Saw in America, London 1922

NO 'RETURN TO NATURE'

Properly speaking, of course, there is no such thing as a return to nature, because there is no such thing as a departure from it. The phrase reminds one of the slightly intoxicated gentleman who gets up in his own dining room and declares firmly that he must be getting home.

Chesterton Review, August 1993

UNDERSTANDING THROUGH INCOMPREHENSION

We have never even begun to understand a people until we have found something that we do not understand. So long as we find the character easy to read, we are reading into it our own character.

What I Saw in America, London 1922

IT'S ALL RELATIVE

The Red Queen, when she made the famous remark, 'I have seen hills compared with which that would be a valley', stated something which corresponds roughly to what most people mean by Relativity.

The Illustrated London News, 31 January 1931

QUALIFIED FREEDOM

What we call emancipation is always and of necessity simply the free choice of the soul between one set of limitations and another.

Daily News, 21 December 1905

SUITS YOU, MADAM

A woman's clothes never suit her so well as when they seem to suit her by accident.

Manalive, 1915

THE SUN

It has been arrested by Joshua, worshipped by Julian, theorized about by Copernicus, quarrelled about by Galileo, pointed at by Napoleon, put in its proper place by Newton, and seriously disturbed and doubted about by Einstein.

The Illustrated London News, 11 July 1931

A GENT

He is a perfect gentleman; that is his complaint. He does not impose his creed, but simply his class.

Manalive, London 1915

DISCRETION THE BETTER PART OF AMOUR

In one sense, everything about everyone is interesting. But not everybody can interest everybody else: and it is well to know an author is loved, but not to publish all the love-letters.

Robert Louis Stevenson, London 1907

TAKEN TO WHEN TAKEN OFF

By his solemnity [Dickens] commands us to love our neighbours. By his caricature he makes us love them.

Introduction to Dickens's *The Old Curiosity Shop*, London 1907

ELIZABETH BARRETT BROWNING

She often took the step from the sublime to the ridiculous; but to take this step one must reach the sublime.

Robert Browning, London 1903

CALEDONIAN CONFIDENTIAL

. . . The Scots are secret sentimentalists and cannot always keep the secret.

Robert Louis Stevenson, London 1907

ON THE FENCE

Impartiality is a pompous name for indifference, which is an elegant name for ignorance.

The Speaker, 15 December 1900

WAKE-UP CALL

A land that is a sleeping beauty exists to be woken up; and it is as well for her if she can be woken up by a lover before she is woken up by an enemy.

The Illustrated London News, 1 September 1923

SO THERE, DR FREUD

Psycho-analysis is the Confessional without the safeguards of the Confessional . . .

The Thing, New York 1930

COMPARATIVE RELIGIONS

We have practically come to a condition in which Christianity is the only religion which Christians do not study.

The Illustrated London News, 7 July 1928

THE REASON WHY

On the whole, I am rather less interested in what people do, than in why they do it.

The Illustrated London News, 1 December 1928

WHAT WE WOT NOT OF

A social system is always destroyed by the thing that it does not understand – the thing that it has too long left out of account.

The Illustrated London News, 18 February 1928

UMBERSTANDABLE

I used to be puzzled by the name of 'raw umber', being unable to imagine the effect of fried umber or stewed umber. But the colours of New York are exactly in that key . . .

What I Saw in America, London 1922

SECOND NATURE

We can say, if we like, that it is natural to be artificial.

The Illustrated London News, 7 January 1928

GKC continues that argument by suggesting that when man tries to be natural 'the hairy animals will always outstrip him'.

BRIEF CHRONICLES

Granted that the old formal folios of epic and tragedy were too formal, it sometimes looks nowadays as if there would be no books except note-books or sketch-books.

The Illustrated London News, 21 May 1932

STREET-WISE

A street is really more poetical than a meadow, because a street has a secret. A street is going somewhere, and a meadow nowhere.

The Napoleon of Notting Hill, London 1904

Tasters

THE LAUGH'S ON ME

It is unpardonable conceit not to laugh at your own jokes.

'The Flat Freak', *Alarms and Discursions*, London 1911

OLD WIVES' TALES

I would always trust the old wives' fables against the old maids' facts.

Orthodoxy, London 1909

AGAINST THE CURRENT

A dead thing can go with the stream, but only a living thing can go against it.

The Everlasting Man, London 1925

THE ROAD TO UTOPIA

Whether or no the world is travelling towards the right goal, it seems to me to have almost invariably taken the wrong turning . . . Utopia has been something always near and never discovered.

The Illustrated London News, 27 April 1929

BORINGLY RIGHT

. . . There must always be monotony in advice while there is consistency in policy.

The Illustrated London News, 26 October 1918

CLEARING THE DECKS

Any one setting out to dispute anything ought always to begin by saying what he does not dispute.

Orthodoxy, London 1909

SMALL IS NOT NECESSARILY BEAUTIFUL

In a large community we can choose our companions. In a small community our companions are chosen for us.

Heretics, London 1906

IN COMMON

The common things of men infinitely outclass all classes.

Fancies versus Fads, London 1923

FISCAL DRAG

A citizen can hardly distinguish between a tax and a fine, except that the fine is generally much lighter.

The Illustrated London News, 25 May 1931

NO SKY SCRAPED

The tall building is itself artistically akin to the tall story. The very word skyscraper is an admirable example of an American lie.

What I Saw in America, London 1922

ME TARZAN, EUGENICS

. . . The experiments in eugenics and criminology already being permitted in America smell more and more of the mad-house.

GK's Weekly, 13 November 1926

ON SHOW

GKC had been on a lecture tour of the United States.

Some say that people come to see the lecturer and not to hear him; in which case it seems rather a pity that he should disturb and distress their minds with a lecture. He might merely display himself on a stand or platform for a stipulated sum; or be exhibited like a monster in a menagerie. The circus elephant is not expected to make a speech.

What I Saw in America, London 1922

A LITTLE TOUCHED

. . . The really sane man knows that he has a touch of the madman.

Orthodoxy, London 1909

MODEL WEATHER

The great English landscape painters . . . paint portraits of the Weather. The Weather sat to Constable. The Weather posed for Turner; and a deuce of a pose it was.

'The Glory of Grey', *Alarms and Discursions*, London 1911

ARK *DE TRIOMPHE*

Recent discoveries in the Near East had 'greatly strengthened the traditional story of the Flood'.

The little wooden Ark of the toy-shop has defeated the vast mysterious Ark of the tradition . . .

The Illustrated London News, 20 April 1929

HYPNOTIC

. . . Hypnotism, like everything else, is a matter of degree; it enters slightly into all daily conversation: it is not necessarily conducted by a man in evening-dress on a platform in a public hall.

'The Miracle of Moon Crescent' (*The Father Brown Stories*)

BLASPHEMY

Blasphemy depends upon belief, and is fading with it. If any one doubts this, let him sit down seriously and try to think blasphemous thoughts about Thor. I think his family will find him at the end of the day in a state of some exhaustion.

Heretics, London 1906

FUNNY, YES; WRONG, NO

. . . Nobody should be ashamed of thinking a thing funny because it is foreign, but he should be ashamed of thinking it wrong because it is funny.

What I Saw in America, London 1922

UNCOMMON SENSE

It is unfortunate that common-sense has come to mean almost the contrary of the sense that is common.

The Illustrated London News, 12 January 1929

ALWAYS THE PERFECT CAVEMAN

Don't say (O don't say) that Primitive Man knocked down a woman with a club and carried her away. Why on earth should he? Does the male sparrow knock down the female sparrow with a twig? Does the male giraffe knock down the female giraffe with a palm tree?

A Miscellany of Men, London 1912

ON BELIEF

It seems a mere mad negation to start from scratch.

The Illustrated London News, 3 April 1926

BIOGRAPHY

GKC is assessing — mainly favourably — a new life of William Cobbett by G. D. H. Cole.

It keeps to almost exactly the right extent the difficult task of the biographer. I mean the task of being both inside and outside the hero.

The Illustrated London News, 4 July 1925

SUCH SWEET SORROW

All creation is separation. Birth is as solemn a parting as death.

Orthodoxy, London 1909

JOBSWORTH

On Victorian lady watercolourists.

If a thing is worth doing, it is worth doing badly.

What's Wrong with the World, London 1910

2
LITERATURE

SHAKESPEARE

. . . The thing which has puzzled so many dilettante critics [is] the problem of the extreme ordinariness of the behaviour of so many great geniuses in history. Their behaviour was so ordinary that it was not recorded; hence it was so ordinary that it seemed mysterious. Hence people say that Bacon wrote Shakespeare. The modern artistic temperament cannot understand how a man who could write such lyrics as Shakespeare wrote, could be as keen as Shakespeare was on business transactions in a little town in Warwickshire. The explanation is simple enough; it is that Shakespeare had a real lyrical impulse, wrote a real lyric, and so got rid of the impulse and went about his business. Being an artist did not prevent him from being an ordinary man . . .

Heretics, London 1906

AN ARDEN IS A LOVESOME THING

It is well that those who are sick with love or sick with the absence of love, those who weary of the folly of courts or weary yet more of their wisdom, it is natural that these should trail away into the twinkling twilight of the woods. Yet it is here that Shakespeare makes one of his most arresting and startling assertions of the truth. Here is one of those rare and tremendous moments of which one may say that there is a stage direction, 'Enter Shakespeare'. He has admitted that for men weary of courts, for men sick of cities, the wood is the wisest place, and he has praised it with his purest lyric ecstasy. But when a man comes suddenly upon that celestial picnic, a man who is not sick of cities, but sick of hunger, a man who is not weary of courts, but weary of walking, then Shakespeare lets through his own voice with a shattering sincerity and cries the praise of practical human civilization:

> If ever you have looked on better days,
> If ever you have sat at good men's feasts,
> If ever been where bells have knolled to church,
> If ever from your eyelids wiped a tear
> Or know what 'tis to pity and be pitied.

There is nothing finer even in Shakespeare than that conception of the circle of rich men all pretending to rough it in the country, and the one really hungry man entering, sword in hand, and praising the city. 'If ever you have been where bells have knolled to church'; if you have ever been within sound of Bow bells; if you have ever been happy and haughty enough to call yourself a Cockney.

Introduction to Dickens's *A Tale of Two Cities*, London 1909

THE SECRET SHAKESPEARE

Shakespeare did, for the first and last time, really wish to put himself beyond the reach of the Shakespearean critics. Shakespeare did really wish to leave behind him one real cryptogram; not a silly alphabetical cypher to say that he was Francis Bacon or Queen Elizabeth or the Earl of Southampton; but something to say that he was the Shakespeare whom we shall never know. As if he had been suddenly alarmed at the horrid notion that he had really unlocked his heart with the key of the Sonnets as Wordsworth suggested; and had then resolved to leave behind him a casket that no key can unlock.

The Illustrated London News, 11 January 1936

WELL STOLEN

If it be hopeless to denounce Shakespeare, it may appear almost as impertinent to defend him. And yet there is one point on which he never has been defended. And it is one on which I think he should not only be defended, but admired.

If I were a Shakespearean student . . . I should plead for the merit of Shakespeare's plots; all the more because they were somebody else's plots. In short, I should say a word for the poet's taste; if only his taste in theft . . . Shakespeare *enjoyed* the old stories. He enjoyed them as tales are intended to be enjoyed. He liked reading them. . .

Nearly all the critics apologise, in a prim and priggish manner, for the tale on which turns the Trial Scene in 'The Merchant of Venice'. They explain that poor Shakespeare had taken a barbarous old story, and had to make the best of it. As a matter of fact he had taken an uncommonly good story; one of the best that he could possibly have had to make the best of. It is a clear, pointed, and practical parable against usury.

The Illustrated London News, 18 October 1919

PERCHANCE NOT TO DREAM

We cannot have a Midsummer Night's Dream if our one object in life is to keep ourselves awake with the black coffee of criticism.

'A Midsummer Night's Dream', The Common Man, London 1950

ROMEO AND JULIET

. . . What a man learns from 'Romeo and Juliet' is not some theory of sex; it is the mystery of something much more than what sensualists call Sex, and what cads call Sex Appeal. What he learns from 'Romeo and Juliet' is not to call first love 'calf love'; not to call even fleeting love a flirtation, but to understand that these things, which a million vulgarians have vulgarized, are not vulgar. The great poet exists to show the small man how great he is.

Chaucer, London 1932

BARD BARRED

I have heard a story . . . to the effect that the French Academy accepted the accident of the absence of Molière from its records with a magnificent gesture . . . [It] erected in its inner courts a special statue of Molière, with the inscription: '*Rien ne manque à sa gloire; il manque à la nôtre*' . . . and if you want to know what is the difference between the atmosphere of France and England . . . you have only to imagine anybody making, or even anybody suggesting, a public apology of that sort to Shakespeare. Can you imagine a huge statue of Shakespeare in Balliol Quad, inscribed with the statement: 'Shakespeare never went to Balliol'?

GK's Weekly, 2 May 1935

JOHN MILTON

GKC thought that Milton was the one poet to whom one could honourably apply the term 'art for art's sake' which he (GKC) had abominated in his youth.

It does really seem to me that Milton was an artist, and nothing but an artist; and yet so great an artist as to sustain by his own strength the idea that art can exist alone. He seems to me an almost solitary example of a man of magnificent genius whose greatness does not depend at all upon moral morality. His greatness is in a style, and a style which seems to me rather unusually separate from its substance. What is the exact nature of the pleasure which I, for one, take in reading and repeating some such lines, for instance, as those familiar ones:

> Dying put on the weeds of Dominic
> Or in Franciscan think to pass disguised.

So far as I can see, the whole effect is in a certain unexpected order and arrangement of words, independent and distinguished, like the perfect manners of an eccentric gentleman. Say instead 'Put on in death the weeds of Dominic', and the whole unique dignity of the line has broken down. It is something in the quiet but confident inversion of 'Dying put on' which exactly achieves that perpetual slight novelty which Aristotle profoundly said was the language of poetry.

Fancies versus Fads, London 1923

JOHN DRYDEN

We have all heard people cite the celebrated line of Dryden as 'Great genius is to madness near allied'. But Dryden did not say that great genius was to madness near allied. Dryden was a great genius himself, and knew better . . . What Dryden said was this, 'Great wits are oft to madness near allied': and that is true. It is the pure promptitude of the intellect that is in peril of a breakdown.

Orthodoxy, London 1909

THE ALLURE OF CRUSOE

The charm of Robinson Crusoe is not in the fact that he could find his way to a remote island, but in the fact that he could not find any way of getting away from it. It is that fact which gives an intensive interest to all the things that he had with him on the island; the axe and the parrot and the guns, and the little hoard of grain.

The Illustrated London News, 8 February 1930

PULVERIZED

. . . Johnson did not really specialize in speaking Johnsonese. The very Johnsonian sentences that are sometimes quoted were almost invariably picked and placed for the deliberate purpose of pulverizing some pompous ass with an elaborate exactitude.

The Illustrated London News, 4 April 1936

DR JOHNSON, WE PRESUME

GKC had taken part in a pageant. The illustration of GKC as Dr Johnson (p. xxxvi) relates to this.

This old pageant included a series of figures from the eighteenth century, and I was told that I was just like Dr Johnson. Seeing that Dr Johnson was heavily seamed with small-pox, had a waistcoat all over gravy, snorted and rolled as he walked, and was probably the ugliest man in London, I mention this identification as a fact and not as a vaunt . . . I requested that a row of posts should be erected across the lawn, so that I might touch all of them but one, and then go back and touch that. Failing this, I felt that the least they could do was to have twenty-five cups of tea stationed at regular intervals along the course, each held by a Mrs Thrale in full costume.

Tremendous Trifles, London 1909

TOM JONES A MORAL BOOK

In 1907 – the bicentenary of Henry Fielding's birth – GKC was indignant when journalists writing about the novelist apologized for the 'immorality' of his work, especially of his picaresque novel Tom Jones.

The truth is that all these things mark a change in the general view of morals; not, I think, a change for the better. We have grown to associate morality in a book with a kind of optimism and prettiness; according to us, a moral book is a book about moral people. But the old idea was almost exactly the opposite; a moral book was a book about immoral people. A moral book was full of pictures like Hogarth's 'Gin Lane' or 'Stages of Cruelty', or it recorded, like the popular broadsheet, 'God's dreadful judgement' against some blasphemer or murderer . . . If Tom Jones violated morality, so much the worse for Tom Jones.

'Tom Jones and Morality', *All Things Considered*, London 1908

GRAY'S ELEGY

. . . Something was, indeed, fading before the eyes of Thomas Gray, the poet, and it was something that he did not wish to see fade. It may be noted that the first impression, especially in the first verses, is one of things moving away from the poet and leaving him alone. We see only the back of the plough-man, so to speak, as he plods away into the darkness; the herds of cattle have the perspective of vanishing things; for a whole world was indeed passing out of the sight and reach of that learned and sensitive and secluded gentleman, who represented the culture of eighteenth-century England, and could only watch a twilight transformation which he could not understand. For when the ploughman comes back out of that twilight, he will come back different. He will be either a scientific works-manager or an entirely new kind of agrarian citizen, great as in the first days of Rome; a free peasant or a servant of alien machinery; but never the same again.

The Illustrated London News, 30 July 1932

THOMAS GRAY

Gray wrote at the very beginning of a certain literary epoch of which we, perhaps, stand at the very end. He represented that softening of the Classic which slowly turned it into the Romantic. We represent that ultimate hardening of the Romantic which has turned it into the Realistic.

The Illustrated London News, 30 July 1932

TRISTRAM SHANDY

A man who has missed the fact that *Tristram Shandy* is a game of digressions, that the whole book is a kind of practical joke to cheat the reader out of a story, simply has not read *Tristram Shandy* at all.

Robert Browning, London 1903

WILLIAM COWPER

. . . The only one great English poet [who] went mad, Cowper . . . was definitely driven mad by logic, by the ugly and alien logic of predestination. Poetry was not the disease, but the medicine; poetry partly kept him in health . . . He was damned by John Calvin; he was almost saved by John Gilpin.

Orthodoxy, London 1909

VERSE FIT FOR HEROES

Two hundred years ago . . . an English poet would sit down with the laudable intention of writing a long didactic poem on the correct cultivation of onions, or the most advisable construction of pig-sties; all set forth in beautiful rhymed decasyllabics, brightened by entirely original selections from the Georgics and decorated by many fine flights of mythological fancy, about Ceres spreading her maternal mantle over the first onion, or Circe standing amid her pig-sties of ivory and gold. Everybody knows that the very latest poetical style has gone to the other extreme, and is not only brief, but abrupt.

The Illustrated London News, 21 May 1932

SKIPPING A CENTURY

New movements in literature are those which copy the last century but one. If they copy the last century, they are old-fashioned; but if it is quite clear that they are much more than a hundred years old, they are entirely fresh and original . . . The Romantics of the nineteenth century were appealing back to the more purely poetical poets of the seventeenth century, against the almost prosaical poets of the eighteenth century. Indeed, Romanticism, though it so often went with Revolutionism, was in its very nature a more general appeal to the past. Perhaps the most genuinely and practically effective popularist of the new Romanticism was Sir Walter Scott, whose truest title is The Antiquary . . . Even Byron was always looking backward, and he died not for the modern Liberals, but for the ancient Greeks.

. . . The same is true of the twentieth century; and the twentieth century also is copying the last century but one. In short, it is copying the eighteenth century, and especially all that was most hated and condemned in the work of the eighteenth century . . . [Twentieth-century writers] especially imitate . . . its coarseness and its coldness . . .

Mr Aldous Huxley much more closely suggests a return to Swift than an extension of Yeats . . . The ruthlessness of *Brave New World* is . . . like the ruthlessness of *Gulliver's Travels*.

The Illustrated London News, 19 May 1934

ROBERT BURNS

There is nothing in God's earth that really expresses the bottom of the nature of a man in love except Burns's songs. To the man not in love they must seem inexplicably simple. When he says, 'My love is like the melody that's sweetly played in tune', it seems almost a crude way of referring to music. But a man in love with a woman feels a nerve move suddenly that Dante groped for and Shakespeare hardly touched.

Letter to his fiancée, Frances Blogg, 14 July 1899

COLERIDGE

He was a great Character; one of those men of whom numberless anecdotes are told, chiefly to the effect that his conversation
was fascinating and continuous; some even found it too continuous. There is the famous story of the man whom Coleridge
buttonholed in the street and proceeded to talk to about Plato
at some length; whereupon the man, having an appointment,
delicately and tactfully cut off the button and went about his
business. Returning later by the same street, he saw Coleridge
still holding the button and still talking about Plato.

'About S.T.C.', *As I Was Saying*, London 1936

WALTER SAVAGE LANDOR

He had the double arrogance which is only possible to that old
and stately but almost extinct blend – the aristocratic republican. Like an old Roman senator, or like a gentleman of the
Southern States of America, he had the condescension of a
gentleman to those below him, combined with the jealous
self-assertiveness of a Jacobin to those above. The only person
who appears to have been able to manage him and bring out
his more agreeable side was Browning . . . Landor, who could
hardly conduct an ordinary business interview without beginning to break the furniture, was fond of Browning.

Robert Browning, London 1903

NOT EVEN GOOD IN PARTS?

The public is not an ass. It appreciates great geniuses much
better than great geniuses appreciate each other. Browning, I
think, referred to Byron's poetry as an addled egg, and what

Byron would have said about Browning's poetry, I simply do not dare to dream.

The Illustrated London News, 12 July 1913

SNAKES ALIVE!

It needs intelligence to weave the pattern; it also needs intelligence to unweave the pattern. A sentence of Ruskin or De Quincey may be as long and sometimes seem as languid as a serpent; it may be figured with elaborate tint and pattern like a serpent. But it is alive and it can strike as swiftly as a serpent. It is all one thing; it has a head and a tail. It is quite different from a worm broken up into writhing bits, of which we can no longer make head or tail.

The Illustrated London News, 14 January 1928

SHELLEY

Nobody could be more entirely in the air, to all appearance, than Shelley. Nothing could be more entirely in the air than his little pet, the Skylark. And no mind could be more filled with the conviction that it was completely in revolt against all tradition, and especially against all religion. And yet it would be quite an amusing exercise to take Shelley's poem about the skylark, line by line and verse by verse, and show how entirely dependent it is upon traditional ideas, and even rather specially upon religious ideas . . . The song of the radiant young Atheist would probably turn out in the end to be a most orthodox theological tract. He begins by saying, 'Hail to thee, blithe spirit.' What does he mean by talking about spirits, if he is not in any sense a spiritualist? What would be the meaning of the remark, if he were really a materialist? He then says, 'Bird thou never wert', which is obviously a lie. But it is a lie symbolising a truth, and what he really means may be stated thus: 'I refuse to believe that a bird is only a bird, or that there is nothing more in such things than the material facts that we know about them.' That thought is the beginning of all theology.

The Illustrated London News, 13 October 1920

WORD THOU NEVER WERT

. . . Language has been from the dawn of the world reserved for two purposes, which may be simplified into the two divisions of poetry and prose . . . Poetry simply consists of connotation. It is all in the atmosphere created by the terms, as an incantation calls up spirits. It is almost more made up of the echoes of words than the words themselves. It is not really even the images, but the haloes around the images. 'Of perilous seas in faery lands forlorn' does not owe its effect to the assertion, as on an Admiralty chart, that certain seas are dangerous for navigators.

The Illustrated London News, 8 January 1927

A SUBURBAN VIRGIL

Tennyson, of course, owed a great deal to Virgil. There is no question of plagiarism here; a debt to Virgil is like a debt to Nature. But Tennyson was a provincial Virgil. In such passages as that about the schoolboy's barring out he might be called a suburban Virgil. I mean that he tried to have the universal balance of all the ideas at which the great Roman had aimed; but he hadn't got hold of all the ideas to balance. Hence his work was not a balance of truths, like the universe. It was a balance of whims; like the British Constitution.

The Victorian Age in Literature, London 1913

AN ORNAMENTAL EXTINGUISHER

It is interestingly true of Tennyson's philosophical temper that he was almost the only Poet Laureate who was not ludicrous. It is not absurd to think of Tennyson as tuning his harp in praise of Queen Victoria: that is, it is not absurd in the sense as Chaucer's harp hallowed by dedication to Richard II or Wordsworth's harp hallowed by dedication to George IV is absurd . . . If Dickens is Cobbett's destiny stirring in the grave, Tennyson is the exquisitely ornamental extinguisher on the flame of the first revolutionary poets. England has settled down; England has become Victorian.

The Victorian Age in Literature, London 1913

TENNYSON AND BROWNING

It is not true that Tennyson was more of a poet than Browning, if we mean by that statement that Browning could not compose forms as artistic and well-managed, lyrics as light and poignant, and rhythms as swelling and stirring as any in English letters. But it is true that Tennyson was more of a poet than Browning, if we mean by that statement that Tennyson was a poet in person, in post and circumstance and conception of life; and that Browning was not, in that sense, a poet at all. Browning first inaugurated in modern art and letters the notion or tradition, in many ways perhaps a more wholesome one, that the fact that a man pursued the trade or practice of poetry was his own affair and a thing apart, like the fact that he collected coins or earned his living as a hatter. But Tennyson really belonged to an older tradition, the tradition that believed that the poet, the appointed 'Vates', was a recognized and public figure like the bard or jester at the medieval courts, like the prophet in the old Commonwealth of Israel. In Tennyson's work appeared for the last time in English history this notion of the stately and public and acknowledged poet: it was the lay of the last minstrel.

G. F. Watts, London 1904

IN A GROOVE

. . . When Tennyson, in a wild and rather weak manner, welcomed the idea of infinite alteration in society, he instinctively took a metaphor which suggests an imprisoned tedium. He wrote: 'Let the great world spin for ever down the ringing grooves of change.' He thought of change itself as an unchangeable groove; and so it is.

Orthodoxy, London 1909

MERCIFUL RELEASES

'You can't really mean, Mr Braintree,' remonstrated the lady, 'that you want great men to be killed.'

'Well, I think there's something in the idea,' said Braintree. 'Tennyson deserved to be killed for writing the May-Queen, and Browning deserved to be killed for rhyming "promise" and "from mice", and Carlyle deserved to be killed for being Carlyle . . . and Dickens deserved to be killed for not killing Little Nell quick enough . . .'

The Return of Don Quixote, London 1927

POE'S 'DARK LUXURY'

The point of Poe is that we feel that *everything* is decaying, including ourselves; faces are already growing featureless like those of lepers; roof-trees are rotting from root to roof; one great grey fungus as vast as a forest is sucking up life rather than giving it forth . . .

Robert Louis Stevenson, London 1907

THE RUBÁIYÁT OF OMAR KHAYYÁM

For more than thirty years the shadow and glory of a great Eastern figure has lain upon our English literature. Fitzgerald's translation of Omar Khayyám concentrated into an immortal poignancy all the dark and drifting hedonism of our time. Of the literary splendour of that work it would be merely banal to speak; in few other of the books of men has there been anything so combining the gay pugnacity of an epigram with the vague sadness of a song. But of its philosophical, ethical, and religious influence, which has been almost as great as its brilliancy, I should like to say a word, and that word, I confess, one of uncompromising hostility . . .

One matter of indictment towers ominously above the rest – a genuine disgrace to it, a genuine calamity to us. This is the terrible blow that this great poem has struck against sociability and the joy of life . . . Omar Khayyám's wine-bibbing is bad, not because it is wine-bibbing. It is bad, and very bad, because it is medical wine-bibbing. It is the drinking of a man who drinks because he is not happy. His is the wine that shuts out the universe, not the wine that reveals it.

Heretics, London 1906

TROLLOPE

What the serious historians have disguised, the frivolous novelist has detected. Their histories are fiction and his fiction is history. That is the truth; and that is Trollope's unconscious

witness to what the Whigs really did in English history . . .
What the [English] Revolution did was . . . to establish certain
great magnates, whose wealth and power were far out of
proportion to those of the ordinary gentleman, let alone the
ordinary citizen. They owned everything, and Trollope knew
it. What other possible meaning is there in the title of *The
Duke of Omnium*?

The Illustrated London News, 15 March 1930

WALT WHITMAN

My whole youth was filled, as with a sunrise, with the san-
guine glow of Walt Whitman. He seemed to me something
like a crowd turned to a giant, or like Adam the First Man. It
thrilled me to hear of somebody who had heard of somebody,
who saw him in the street; it was as if Christ were still alive
. . . I never had a hint of the evil some enemies have attributed
to him; if it was there, it was not there for me. What I saluted
was a new equality which was not a dull levelling but an
enthusiastic lifting; a shouting exultation in the mere fact that
men were men.

The Thing, New York 1930

THE VOICE OF MILLIONS

To one American man of genius, whom I read in my youth,
I owed much of my deliverance from the decadent cynicism
that was corrupting most of the young men of my generation.
Walt Whitman had his faults, artistic and other, but he did
lead the democracy of the 'Leaves of Grass' against the oligarchy of 'The Green Carnation' . . . He sounded like the
voice of a new nation; like the voice of many million men.

The Illustrated London News, 21 April 1928

MEREDITH

It seemed to most of us, in our boyhood, that [George Meredith] was not only the greatest literary artist then present, but that he was prophetically the first literary artist of the future. He was not only the greatest English author alive, but the only English author who would live. And yet he has not really lived; certainly he has not yet really triumphed.

The Illustrated London News, 19 May 1934

BROKEN BOND

George Meredith had just died.

The death of George Meredith is the real end of the Nineteenth Century, not that empty date that came at the close of 1899. The last bond is broken between us and the pride and peace of the Victorian age. Our fathers are all dead. We are suddenly orphans: we all feel strangely and sadly young.

GKC acknowledges that Thomas Hardy (b. 1840) is still alive, but writes that he considers him a 'modern'.

The Illustrated London News, 22 May 1909

WE ARE AMUSED

It seems to me that in many ways it was [the Victorians] who were frivolous and their descendants who are serious . . . The light nonsense of the nineteenth century anticipated so much of the heavy nonsense of the twentieth. Lewis Carroll did identically the same thing [as James Joyce and Gertrude Stein], only he happened to know it was funny, and therefore he did it for fun.

The Illustrated London News, 12 September 1931

Illustration 7: Caricature of Lewis Carroll by Harry Furniss.

Illustration 8: Caricature of Swinburne by Harry Furniss.

SWINBURNE AND CHRISTIANITY

I rolled on my tongue with a terrible joy, as did all young men of that time, the taunts which Swinburne hurled at the dreariness of the creed – 'Thou hast conquered, O pale Galilean, the world has grown gray with Thy breath'.

Orthodoxy, London 1909

WHAT DID SWINBURNE MEAN?

GKC has been reading Edmund Gosse's essay on Swinburne in an anthology of essays edited by Lord Birkenhead.

After reading Gosse's essay again, I asked myself: 'What on earth did Swinburne mean? Or did he mean anything?' It is easy enough, after reading some of his poems . . . to say that he did not mean anything; that he was simply a musician gone wrong; a lunatic with something singing in his head; a creature throbbing with suppressed dancing; a creature who could not help foaming at the mouth with flowers and flames and blood and blossoms and the sea. But it is not easy, after reading Gosse's essay, to deny that he did in some way take something seriously . . . He did seem really to believe that some Utopia depended on the success of Cavour or the failure of Louis Bonaparte. But exactly how he connected it in his own mind with the queer licentious pessimism, like the last debauch of a suicide, which fills his . . . verses, I cannot make out . . .

The Illustrated London News, 25 January 1930

LOST LOVE

'I have lived long enough to have seen one thing; that love hath an end': so runs, as everyone will remember, the first line of Swinburne's 'Hymn to Prosperine', the dirge of a Pagan farewell to Paganism. I have lived long enough to have seen one thing: that the love of Swinburne hath an end. Not the admiration for Swinburne, not the reasonable appreciation of Swinburne; but that particular sort of love of Swinburne which is like first love in youth; perhaps (one is sometimes tempted to think) the only sort of real love that Swinburne had ever known anything about. I mean that sort of mere magic spell or enchantment of Swinburne which so many young people had in the period when, as Mr Maurice Baring has very truly said, Swinburne seemed to them not so much the best poet as simply the only poet.

The Illustrated London News, 21 March 1931

HERO-WORSHIPPER

Swinburne had just died.

. . . He has filled pages of prose with really passionate eulogy; and . . . perhaps no poet ever wrote so many good poems in praise of other men. From the high, buoyant outburst to Whitman:

> Send but over a song to us,
> Heart of all hearts that are free

Down to the deep agnostic wail to the dead Landor –

> But thou, if anything endure,
> If hope there be,
> O spirit that man's life left pure,
> Man's death set free. . .

The Illustrated London News, 17 April 1909

RHYME CRIME?

If I told you offhand that a man had rhymed 'Arisbe' to 'kiss be' and 'statue' to 'at you', you would think it grotesque, and merely wonder whether it was Browning or the Bab Ballads. Yet Swinburne's river carries us over those rocks quite easily in the verse of which I quote half:

> That met you of old by the statue
> With a look shot out sharp after thieves
> From the eyes of the garden god at you
> Across the fig-leaves.

The Illustrated London News, 17 April 1909

WALTER PATER

Pater's mistake is revealed in his most famous phrase. He asks us to burn with a hard, gem-like flame. Flames are never hard and never gem-like – they cannot be handled or arranged. So human emotions are never hard and never gem-like; they are always dangerous, like flames, to touch or even to examine.

Heretics, London 1906

THOMAS HARDY

Hardy had just died, aged 88.

Thomas Hardy, the maker of great tragedies, had through all his life learned the noblest lesson of the grand Greek tragedies of whose high thunders his voice was perhaps the last reverberation. He may be called a heathen rather than a heretic; for he was never near enough to Christianity to contradict it. But in none of his contradictions, such as they were, was there anything of that special sort of insolence against which Greek tragedy warned heroes and kings. He was often provocative, but he was never proud.

The Illustrated London News, 21 January 1928

CRUEL NATURE

The great agnostics of the Victorian age said there was no purpose in Nature. Mr Hardy is a mystic; he says there is an evil purpose.

The Illustrated London News, 22 May 1909

HARDY'S 'PRACTICAL JOKES'

His novels and poems are full of a sort of solid antics that stick in the memory almost apart from the meaning. They might be called the practical jokes of a pessimist. A very typical example is the poem about the prodigal who, returning home, thinks he sees his father, the huntsman, afar off, conspicuous by his red coat, when his father has long been dead, and the red coat is hung on a scarecrow. That, of course, is very characteristic Hardy in every aspect: the view of life which is something more than tragic irony and approaches sometimes to a sort of torturer's mockery.

The Illustrated London News, 21 January 1928

HARDY'S PESSIMISM

Hardy's pessimism was never really agnosticism. It was not even atheism. It was a strange sort of demoniac monism, which conceived a cosmic centre immediately responsible for the most minute and. remote result of everything, and which he was always reproaching with its responsibility.

The Illustrated London News, 21 January 1928

GERARD MANLEY HOPKINS

[The moral of the Victorian age] is rather a warning against being unconventional than merely against being conventional. We have many odd writers, writing in odd styles, in our own time; they may or may not retain influence in later times. But I cannot remember a single Victorian with an odd style whose odd style is now of any advantage to him: not Carlyle; not Browning; not Meredith; not Doughty. The one solitary exception I remember, whose name has somewhat floated to the surface again of late, is that of Gerard Hopkins.★

The Illustrated London News, 12 September 1931

★Robert Bridges had brought out an edition of Hopkins's poetry in 1918, almost 30 years after the poet's death. GKC's comment is interesting in that it was published a year before F. R. Leavis praised the Jesuit poet highly in *New Bearings in English Poetry*. Though GKC was not an enthusiast for metrical experiments, he may have been predisposed in favour of Hopkins because the poet was a Roman Catholic priest.

PETER PAN

Peter Pan carries on by lineal tradition the cult of the child, beginning with *Treasure Island*; but if there be anything to criticize in Sir James Barrie's beautiful fantasia, it is that wilder things happen to Wendy in a London nursery than ever happen to Jim in a tropical island.

Robert Louis Stevenson, London 1907

GEORGE MOORE

Mr Moore's egoism is not merely a moral weakness, it is a very constant and influential aesthetic weakness as well. We should really be much more interested in Mr Moore if he were not quite so interested in himself. We feel as if we were being shown through a gallery of really fine pictures, into each of which, by some useless and discordant convention, the artist had represented the same figure in the same attitude. 'The Grand Canal with a distant view of Mr Moore', 'Effect of Mr Moore through a Scotch Mist', 'Mr Moore by Firelight', 'Ruins of Mr Moore by Moonlight', and so on, seems to be the endless series.

Heretics, London 1906

THE IMPORTANCE OF BEING OSCAR

It does sometimes happen that a man of real talent has a weakness for flattery, even the flattery of fools. He would rather say something that silly people think clever than something which only clever people could perceive to be true. Oscar Wilde was a man of this type. When he said somewhere that an immoral woman is the sort of woman a man never gets tired of, he used a phrase so baseless as to be perfectly pointless. Everybody knows that a man may get tired of a whole procession of immoral women, especially if he is an immoral man . . . But when he said, 'A cynic is a man who knows the price of everything and the value of nothing', he made a statement (in excellent epigrammatic form) which really meant something. But it would have meant his own immediate dethronement if it could have been understood by those who only enthroned him for being cynical.

The Thing, New York 1930

THE MARTYRDOM OF WILDE

In the fifteenth century men cross-examined and tormented a man because he preached some immoral attitude; in the nineteenth century we fêted and flattered Oscar Wilde because he preached such an attitude, and then broke his heart in penal servitude because he carried it out.

Heretics, London 1906

FRANCIS THOMPSON

The Roman Catholic poet Francis Thompson died in 1907.

With Francis Thompson we lose the greatest poetic energy since Browning. . . Great poets use the telescope and also the microscope. Great poets are obscure for two opposite reasons; now, because they are talking about something too large for any one to understand, and now again because they are talking about something too small for any one to see. Francis Thompson possessed both these infinities.

'A Dead Poet', *All Things Considered*, London 1908

RUDYARD KIPLING

That genuine Anglo-Indian magician, Mr Rudyard Kipling, was brought up in a land of spells and trances, of glaring and tropical illusions. He has been called a realist; and this is true in one sense, but entirely untrue in the other. If realism means an astonishing genius for making things seem real, Mr Kipling is, or has been, a great realist. If it means caring a button whether things are real or not, he never has been and never could be. The East is in him; the glamour of that self-deception that floats thinly on a sea of despair. Vividness has nothing to do with truth; in fact, truth often tends to look a little misty and atmospheric. It is the lies that glow and glare and impose themselves.

The Illustrated London News, 19 November 1910

PHILANDERER OF THE NATIONS

[Kipling] is a perfect master of that light melancholy with which a man looks back on having been the citizen of many communities, of that light melancholy with which a man looks back on having been the lover of many women. He is the philanderer of the nations.

Heretics, London 1906

H. G. WELLS

There is one thing which critics perhaps tend to forget when they complain that Mr H. G. Wells no longer concerns himself with telling a story. It is that nobody else could interest and excite us so much without telling a story.

The Illustrated London News, 15 July 1922

PROGNOSTICATIONS

The modern man no longer preserves the memoirs of his great-grandfather, but he is engaged in writing a detailed and authoritative biography of his great-grandson . . . Sir Walter Scott stands at the dawn of the nineteenth century for the novel of the past; Mr H. G. Wells stands at the dawn of the twentieth century for the novel of the future.

What's Wrong with the World, London 1910

ARNOLD BENNETT

GKC had just read an article on 'the religious doctrines of Mr Arnold Bennett'.

. . . The prominence in the press of this name in this connection is one of the standing mysteries of modern journalism. I have not only a great admiration for the artistic genius, but in many ways a strong liking for the human personality of Mr Arnold Bennett. I like his liveliness and contempt for contempt. I like his humanity and merciful curiosity about every thing human. I like that essential absence of snobbishness that enables him to sympathize even with snobs. But talking about the religious beliefs of Mr Arnold Bennett seems to me exactly like talking about the fox-hunting adventures of Mr Bernard Shaw . . . or the monastic vows of Mr Bertrand Russell. Mr Arnold Bennett has never disguised, as it seems to me, the essential fact that he has not got any religious beliefs . . .

The Thing, New York 1930

HILAIRE BELLOC

[I could give a long list] of topics on which he was opposed to everyone else's opinion and sometimes opposed to mine. To mention only a few things, large and small, he would probably be the only person in a drawing-room saying that Lewis Carroll was overrated, that Byron and Longfellow were not overrated, that wit is superior to humour, that *Ally Sloper's Half-Holiday* was superior to *Punch*, that James the Second was chiefly notable as a stolid English patriot suspicious of French influence; that an Irish political murder might actually be excusable as a Russian political murder (old regime) . . . that it is the mark of the Protestant culture to tolerate Catholicism and the mark of the Catholic culture to persecute it . . .

The Thing, New York 1930

THEODORE DREISER

I have . . . respectfully declined to read all the colossal volumes of Mr Dreiser (admittedly somewhat heavy in style) solely for the pleasure of learning that Mr Dreiser has found life dull and senseless; or, in other words, that Mr Dreiser has never found life at all.★

The Illustrated London News, 21 April 1928

★Theodore Herman Albert Dreiser (1871–1945), American novelist. He was born in Terre Haute, Indiana, the eleventh child of a poor Roman Catholic German immigrant father. At fifteen he left home for Chicago. He became a successful journalist and in 1900 published *Sister Carrie*, a rags-to-riches story of a working-class girl. His best known novel is *An American Tragedy* (1925).

DREARY DREISER

He describes a world which appears to be a dull and discolouring illusion of indigestion, not bright enough to be called a nightmare; smelly, but not even stinking with any strength; smelling of the stale gas of ignorant chemical experiments by dirty, secretive schoolboys – the sort of boys who torture cats in corners; spineless and spiritless like a broken-backed worm; loathsomely slow and laborious like an endless slug; despairing, but not with dignity; blaspheming, but not with courage; without wit, without will, without laughter or uplifting of the heart; too old to die, too deaf to leave off talking, too blind to stop, too stupid to start afresh, too dead to be killed, and incapable even of being damned, since in all its weary centuries it has not reached the age of reason.

The Thing, New York 1930

LYTTON STRACHEY

The late Lytton Strachey was to me always rather a mystery, though nobody would mistake him for a mystic. I wallowed, as did all the world, in the wit and style of *Eminent Victorians*, and his special power of picking out a devastating detail, as when he withered all the aesthetic world of Victoria and Albert with the two words 'tartan linoleum'. His Voltairean philosophy did not shock me like flashes of lightning, as it seems to have done some simple persons, for it seems to me as obvious and ordinary as daylight. It is simply insufficient or inadequate; and might be compared to daylight without sunlight.

GK's Weekly, 13 February 1932

D. H. LAWRENCE AND STEPHEN McKENNA

I am very glad that our fashionable fiction seems to be full of a return to paganism, for it may possibly be the first step of a return to Christianity . . . Mr D. H. Lawrence gives us a story about modern people serving the old heathen ritualism of Mexico [in *The Plumed Serpent*]; and Mr Stephen McKenna gives us a study of modern people being stirred again by the heathen hilarity of Pan [*The Oldest God*].

The Illustrated London News, 20 March 1926

T. S. ELIOT

Swinburne was quite certain that he and the world were galloping nearer and nearer to the new Republic and farther and farther from the old Church. If he had been right, it would follow that, by this time, a man like Mr Eliot would be even more Republican than Swinburne. As a matter of fact,

Mr Eliot has actually walked out of a real live Republic and loudly announced that he is a Royalist. He has also declared himself an Anglo-Catholic . . .

The Illustrated London News, 21 March 1931

THE SITWELLS

The literary world is kept in a perpetual brawl about the brothers Sitwell and their distinguished sister. But if we ask what the row is all about, we find it is about poems which describe, especially at their best, the quaint quietude of Early Victorian rooms and gardens and the depth of long childish days.

The Illustrated London News, 18 August 1928

SACHEVERELL SITWELL AND ALDOUS HUXLEY

I could guess what [Beachcomber's] taste would be about most authors,* though I would not always agree with him about the new authors. But I could not guess anything about the tastes of the new authors. If Mr Sacheverell Sitwell suddenly said that the dream of his life would be to murder Whistler or Rossetti, if Mr Aldous Huxley happened to declare that Chopin is a torture to him, I should have an indescribable feeling that they only spoke for themselves. It would not make any difference to my regard for Mr Huxley; but it also would not make any difference to my regard for Chopin . . . It is typical of the situation that I have no notion whether the cat of caprice, in either of these cases, would, in fact, jump towards Chopin or Whistler or away from them.

The Illustrated London News, 4 July 1931

*As already mentioned, the 'Beachcomber' column in the *Daily Express* was started in 1923 by J. B. Morton (1893–1979), a Roman Catholic.

NURSERY VERSERY

On nursery rhymes.

If I were asked to quote four lines which sufficed to illustrate what has been called the imaginative reason, when it rises almost to touch an imaginative unreason (for that point of contact is poetry), I should be content to quote four lines that were in a picture book in my own nursery:

> The man in the wilderness asked of me,
> 'How many strawberries grow in the sea?'
> I answered him, as I thought good:
> 'As many red herrings as grow in the wood.'

Everything in that is poetical; from the dark unearthly figure of the man in the desert, with his mysterious riddles, to the perfect blend of logic and vision which makes beautiful pictures even in proving them impossible.

Illustrated London News, 15 October 1921

BEFORE GRAHAM GREENE WROTE ANY NOVELS

God moves in a mysterious way; and considering that most people would expect Catholic literature to be rather romantic, it will be very amusing if the new Catholic literature turns out to be strictly realistic, and beats the realists at their own game.

Letter to Maurice Baring, 2 July 1924. British Library Add. MSS 73276A

MARKING DOWN

In the great days of Stevenson critics had begun to be ashamed of being critics, and of giving to their ancient function the name of criticism. It was the fashion to publish a book that was a bundle of reviews and to call it 'Appreciations'. But the world advances; and if that sort of book is published now, it might well bear the general title of 'Depreciations'.

Robert Louis Stevenson, London 1907

OBSCURITY IN VERSE

There is a certain kind of fascination, a strictly artistic fascination, which arises from a matter being hinted at in such a way as to leave a certain tormenting uncertainty even at the end. It is well sometimes to half understand a poem in the same manner that we half understand the world.

Robert Browning, London 1903

WHAT POETRY IS

Poetry deals entirely with those great eternal and mainly forgotten wishes which are the ultimate despots of existence. Poetry presents things as they are to our emotions, not as they are to any theory, however plausible, or any argument, however conclusive. If love is in truth a glorious vision, poetry will say that it is a glorious vision, and no philosophers will persuade poetry to say that it is the exaggeration of the instinct of sex.

Robert Browning, London 1903

PRIVATE FACES IN PUBLIC PLACES

GKC is commenting on the publication – deplored by some – of the love-letters of Robert Browning and Elizabeth Barrett.

I am not prepared to admit that there is or can be, properly speaking, in the world anything that is too sacred to be known. That spiritual beauty and spiritual truth are in their nature communicable, and that they should be communicated, is a principle which lies at the root of every conceivable religion. Christ was crucified upon a hill, and not in a cavern, and the word Gospel itself involves the same idea as the ordinary name of a daily paper. Whenever, therefore, a poet or any similar type of man can, or conceives that he can, make all men partakers in some splendid secret of his own heart, I can imagine nothing saner and nothing manlier than his course in doing so . . . But the one essential which exists in all such cases . . . is that the man in question believes that he can make the story as stately to the whole world as it is to him, and he chooses his words to that end. Yet when a work contains expressions which have one value and significance when read by the people to whom they were addressed, and an entirely different value and significance when read by anyone else, then the element of the violation of sanctity does arise.

Robert Browning, London 1903

OCCUPATIONAL HAZARD OF BIOGRAPHERS

. . . It is . . . the sin and snare of biographers that they tend to see significance in everything; characteristic carelessness if their hero drops his pipe, and characteristic carefulness if he picks it up again.

Robert Browning, London 1903

UPON MY SOUL

All good writers express the state of their souls, even (as occurs in some cases of very good writers) if it is in a state of damnation.

Introduction to Dickens's *The Old Curiosity Shop*, London 1907

WHAT'S IN A TITLE?

. . . We often find in the title of one of an author's books what might very well stand for a general description of all of them. Thus all Spenser's works might be called *A Hymn to Heavenly Beauty*; or all Mr Bernard Shaw's bound books might be called *You Never Can Tell*. In the same way the whole substance and spirit of Thackeray might be gathered under the general title *Vanity Fair*. In the same way too the whole substance and spirit of Dickens might be gathered under the general title *Great Expectations*.

Introduction to Dickens's *The Old Curiosity Shop*, London 1907

CONVENTION, GOOD: CLICHÉ, BAD

A convention is generally a matter of reserve, and therefore, though the superficial will not see it, a matter of reserve strength. It means that certain secrets are stored up for more than mere secrecy; that they are banked rather than buried. It has something of the spirit that made our fathers, in the days of the great guilds, give to a Craft the name of a Mystery . . . The catchword is the very opposite. The *cliché* is something that has nothing in reserve; that has no second meaning; that soon loses even its first meaning. It is an exploded squib; it is a spent bullet; it is a creature that has gasped out its little life in one pulse of publicity. When it is not born dead, it is born dying.

The Illustrated London News, 14 May 1932

PERVERTED FICTION

Father Brown: 'All things are from God, and above all, reason and imagination and the great gifts of the mind. They are good in themselves; and we must not altogether forget their origin even in their perversion. Now this man had in him a very noble power to be perverted; the power of telling stories. He was a great novelist; only he had twisted his fictive power to practical and to evil ends; to deceiving men with false fact instead of with true fiction.'

'The Curse of the Golden Cross' (*The Father Brown Stories*)

TRYING IT ON

There are dark and morbid moods in which I am tempted to feel that Evil re-entered the world in the form of Essays. The Essay is like the serpent, smooth and graceful and easy of movement, also wavering or wandering. Besides, I suppose that the very word Essay had the original meaning of 'trying it on'. The serpent was in every sense of the word tentative. The tempter is always feeling his way, and finding out how much other people will stand . . . The serpent can strike without claws, as it can run without legs. It is the emblem of all those arts which are elusive, evasive, impressionistic, and shading away from tint to tint.

The Illustrated London News, 16 February 1929

RHYME SUBLIME

. . . While all forms of genuine verse recur, there is in rhyme a sense of return to exactly the same place. All modes of song go forward and backward like the tides of the sea; but in the great sea of Homeric or Virgilian hexameters, the sea that carried the labouring ships of Ulysses and Aeneas, the thunder of the breakers is rhythmic, but the margin of the foam is necessarily irregular and vague. In rhyme there is rather a sense of water poured safely into one familiar well, or (to use a nobler metaphor) of ale poured safely into one familiar flagon.

Fancies versus Fads, London 1923

AN ARROW TO THE HEART

Rhyme corresponds to a melody so simple that it goes straight like an arrow to the heart. It corresponds to a chorus so familiar and obvious that all men can join in it. I am not disturbed by the suggestion that such an arrow of song, when it hits the heart, may entirely miss the head.

Fancies versus Fads, London 1923

THE LAUREL CROWN

. . . It is often said that the office of Poet Laureate is not fitted to our times. This is true; it is perhaps the most compact condemnation of our times . . . Whenever it is suggested that some little modern man of letters, in a tail-coat and trousers, should be solemnly presented with a Crown of Laurel, everybody laughs as if it were a joke. But it is not the Laurel, but the little man, that is a joke . . . Nobody sees anything silly in those leaves when they cluster round the hood of some bust of Dante.

The Illustrated London News, 17 May 1930

The next week, The Illustrated London News *announced the appointment of John Masefield as the new Poet Laureate.*

YOU ARE AWFUL – BUT I LIKE YOU

By a curious confusion, many modern critics have passed from the proposition that a masterpiece may be unpopular to the other proposition that unless it is unpopular it cannot be a masterpiece. It is as if one were to say that because a clever man may have an impediment in his speech, therefore a man cannot be clever unless he stammers.

The Illustrated London News, 19 August 1922

BAD VERSE

He refers to The Stuffed Owl, *the anthology of bad verse compiled by D. B. Wyndham Lewis and Charles Lee.*

Every now and again, after wading through a hubbub of hundreds of words, we find a word that seems to have gone right by accident. We must not complain: nothing in this mortal life is perfect; not even bad poetry.

The Illustrated London News, 18 July 1931

GKC goes on to suggest that there are two questions to ask about bad verse: 'Why do people who are not poets try to write poetry?' and 'Why do people who are poets fail to write poetry?' He considers the second of these more difficult to answer and 'therefore more worth answering'.

CHEAP FICTION

A taste for trash is of great value to the serious sociologist. By reading intellectual fiction we only find out what the intellectuals are saying, and saying somewhat self-consciously. By reading shockers and police novels we find out what the mass of the people are saying – or, what is more important, what

they are not saying. We find out what they assume uncon-
sciously, and therefore do not think it worth while to say.

The Illustrated London News, 11 February 1928

MODERN POETRY

I have never understood why it should be a progress for poetry
to become prosaic.

The Illustrated London News, 30 January 1926

SHAMATEURS

I should like to see a real poet write again in the heroic couplet
of the didactic eighteenth century . . . The brain may be even
more magnificently at work in Shelley or Coleridge than in
Goldsmith or Pope. But it is much easier to be a sham Shelley
than to be a sham Pope.

The Illustrated London News, 27 March 1926

NOVEL IDEA

. . . The novel is the most typical of modern forms. It is typical
of modern forms especially in this, that it is essentially formless.
All the ancient modes or structures of literature were definite
and severe. Any one composing them had to abide by their
rules; they were what their name implied. Thus a tragedy
might be a bad tragedy, but it was always a tragedy. Thus an
epic might be a bad epic, but it was always an epic. Now in
the sense in which there is such a thing as an epic, in that sense
there is no such thing as a novel . . . The difference between

a good epic by Mr John Milton and a bad epic by Mr John Smith was simply the difference between the same thing done well and the same thing done badly. But it was not (for instance) like the difference between [Samuel Richardson's] *Clarissa Harlowe* and [H. G. Wells's] *The Time Machine* . . . If we say that they are both novels we shall certainly be puzzled in that case to say what on earth a novel is.

Introduction to Dickens's *Dombey and Son*, London 1907

NEEDLE, HAYSTACK

Somewhere embedded in every ordinary book are the five or six words for which really all the rest will be written. Some of our enterprising editors who set their readers to hunt for banknotes and missing ladies might start a competition for finding those words in every novel.

Introduction to Dickens's *Dombey and Son*, London 1907

PENNY DREADFULS

Literature and fiction are two entirely different things. Literature is a luxury; fiction is a necessity. A work of art can hardly be too short, for its climax is its merit. A story can never be too long, for its conclusion is merely to be deplored, like the last halfpenny or the last pipelight. And so, while the increase of the artistic conscience tends in more ambitious works to brevity and impressionism, voluminous industry still marks the producer of the true romantic trash. There was no end to the ballads of Robin Hood; there is no end to the volumes about Dick Deadshot and the Avenging Nine . . . The romantic imagination is not specially plebeian: it is simply human.

The Defendant, London 1901

HISTORICAL NOVELS

All important political questions must be settled by duels fought with long rapiers at wayside inns. You must stick to one side of the quarrel; but even in that you must not bring any of the charges that a person of the period might really have brought. For instance, the Court must be perpetually engaged in plotting to stab the bluff Huguenot; but you must not insist that the Huguenot was a Puritan . . . Above all, slap in the very middle of the Wars of Religion, nobody must seem to have any clear idea of what his own religion is about.

The Illustrated London News, 2 August 1913

THE BIRTH OF A POET

Another tattered rhymester in the ring,
With but the old plea to the sneering Schools,
That with him, too, some secret night in spring
Came the old frenzy of a hundred fools . . .

First stanza of the untitled three-stanza prefatory poem in
The Wild Knight and Other Poems, London 1900.

THE VITALITY OF SLANG

The one stream of poetry which is continually flowing is slang. Every day a nameless poet weaves some fairy tracery of popular language . . . The fashionable slang is hardly even a language; it is like the formless cries of animals, dimly indicating certain broad, well-understood states of mind. 'Bored', 'cut up', 'jolly', 'rotten' and so on, are like the words of some tribe of savages whose vocabulary has only twenty of them. If a man of fashion wished to protest against some solecism in another man of fashion, his utterance would be a mere string of set phrases, as lifeless as a string of dead fish. But an omnibus driver (being filled with the Muse) would burst out into a solid literary effort: 'You're a gen'lman, aren't yer . . . yer boots is a lot brighter than yer 'ed . . .' Keats never put into a sonnet so many remote metaphors as a coster puts into a curse.

The Defendant, London 1901

WORD-PLAY

. . . If the extreme logician turns for his emotions to poetry, he is exasperated and bewildered by discovering that the words of his own trade are used in an entirely different meaning. He conceives that he understands the word 'visible', and then finds Milton applying it to darkness, in which nothing is visible. He supposes that he understands the word 'hide', and then finds Shelley talking of a poet hidden in the light.

George Bernard Shaw, London 1910

COUP DE PIED

. . . English excels in certain angular consonants and abrupt terminations that make it extraordinarily effective for the expression of the fighting spirit and a fierce contempt. How fortunate is the condition of the Englishman who can kick people; and how relatively melancholy that of the Frenchman who can only give them a blow of the foot!

William Cobbett, London 1925

ALWAYS TRUE TO FORM

Mr Bernard Shaw is always represented by those who disagree with him and, I fear, also (if such exist) by those who agree with him, as a capering humorist, a dazzling acrobat, a quick-change artist. It is said that he cannot be taken seriously, that he will defend anything or attack anything, that he will do anything to startle and amuse. All this is not only untrue, but it is, glaringly, the opposite of the truth; it is as wild as to say that Dickens had not the boisterous masculinity of Jane Austen. The whole force and triumph of Mr Bernard Shaw lie in the fact that he is a thoroughly consistent man. So far from his power consisting in jumping through hoops or standing on his head, his power consists in holding his own fortress night and day. He puts the Shaw test rapidly and rigorously to everything that happens in heaven or earth. His standard never varies.

Heretics, London 1906

THE OTHER ST GEORGE

I suppose that the English people will always cling to the lovely legend of Shaw scorning them and deriding them, though he actually defended them when all Europe denounced them.

The Illustrated London News, 26 November 1932

HIS HEART

. . . If I had to describe with fairness the character of Mr Bernard Shaw, I could not express myself more exactly than by saying that he has a heroically large and generous heart; but not a heart in the right place.

Orthodoxy, London 1909

ARMS AND THE MAN

He is perhaps a defective character; but he is not a mixed one. All the virtues he has are heroic virtues. Shaw is like the Venus de Milo; all that there is of him is admirable.

George Bernard Shaw, London 1910

FEMINISM

For . . . others, sex equality meant the emancipation of women, which allowed them to be equal to men. For Shaw it mainly meant the emancipation of men, which allowed them to be rude to women.

George Bernard Shaw, London 1910

WOT IT'S RITE TO RITE

. . . Mr Shaw has found himself, led by the . . . mad imp of modernity, on the side of the people who want to have phonetic spelling. The people who want phonetic spelling generally depress the world with tireless and tasteless explanations of how much easier it would be for children or foreign bagmen if 'height' were spelt 'hite'. Now children would curse spelling whatever it was, and we are not going to permit foreign bagmen to improve Shakespeare. Bernard Shaw charged along quite a different line; he urged that Shakespeare himself believed in phonetic spelling, since he spelt his own name in six different ways.

George Bernard Shaw, London 1910

THE FABIAN SOCIETY

Give me the drainpipes of the Fabians rather than the pan pipes of the later poets; the drainpipes have a nicer smell.

George Bernard Shaw, London 1910

THE FLAW IN SHAW

. . . There does run through him this erratic levity . . . It is a sort of cold extravagance; and it has made him all his enemies.

George Bernard Shaw, London 1910

ANOTHER FLAW

The great defect of that fine intelligence is a failure to grasp and enjoy the things commonly called convention and tradition; which are foods upon which all human creatures must feed frequently if they are to live.

George Bernard Shaw, London 1910

CLARION CALL

. . . Shaw takes even pleasure as a duty. In a queer way he seems to see existence as an illusion and yet as an obligation. To every man and woman, bird, beast, and flower, life is a love-call to be eagerly followed. To Bernard Shaw it is merely a military bugle to be obeyed.

George Bernard Shaw, London 1910

NO FAIRIES AT THE BOTTOM OF HIS GARDEN

[Shaw] attempts to connect his somewhat chilly type of super-man with the heroes of the old fairy tales. But [he] should not talk about the fairy tales; for he does not feel them from the inside . . . On all this side of historic and domestic traditions Bernard Shaw is weak and deficient. He does not approach them as fairy tales, as if he were four, but as 'folklore' as if he were forty.

George Bernard Shaw, London 1910

AIN'T A SANTA

Bernard Shaw (I strongly suspect) began to disbelieve in Santa Claus at a discreditably early age . . . When [he] says that Christmas Day is only a conspiracy kept up by poulterers and wine merchants from strictly business motives, then he says something which is not so much false as startlingly and arrest-ingly foolish. He might as well say that the two sexes were invented by jewellers who wanted to sell wedding rings.

George Bernard Shaw, London 1910

MAKING A LONG STORY SHORT

Bernard Shaw . . . is a master of compression; he can put a conception more compactly than any other man alive. It is therefore rather difficult to compress his compression; one feels as if one were trying to extract a beef essence from Bovril.

George Bernard Shaw, London 1910

WAR'S NOT GLORIOUS

Shaw objects not so much to war as to the attractiveness of war . . . Before the temple of Mars Tolstoy stands and thunders 'There shall be no wars'; Bernard Shaw merely murmurs, 'Wars if you must; but for God's sake, not war songs.'

George Bernard Shaw, London 1910

A TARGET WORTHY OF HIS STEEL

[Mr Bernard Shaw] cast about him for something to attack which was not merely powerful or placid, but was unattacked . . . He found the thing: he found the great unassailed English institution – Shakespeare . . . In Shaw's opinion (one might say) the English do not really enjoy Shakespeare or even admire Shakespeare; one can only say, in the strong colloquialism, that they swear by Shakespeare. He is a mere god; a thing to be invoked. And Shaw's whole business was to set up the things which were to be sworn by as things to be sworn at.

George Bernard Shaw, London 1910

HEARING BOTH SIDES

[Shaw] said that one should never tell a child anything without letting him hear the opposite opinion. That is to say, when you tell Tommy not to hit his sick sister on the temple, you must make sure of the presence of some Nietzschean professor, who will explain to him that such a course might possibly serve to eliminate the unfit. When you are in the act of telling Susan not to drink out of the bottle labelled 'poison', you must telegraph for a Christian Scientist, who will be ready to maintain that without her own consent it cannot do her any harm.

George Bernard Shaw, London 1910

UNSHAVIAN

. . . His beard has turned grey; the last to his regret, as he wanted it to remain red till they had completed colour-photography.

George Bernard Shaw, London 1910

3

THE PRESS

ADVICE IGNORED

On the whole, I think I owe my success (as the millionaires say) to having listened respectfully and rather bashfully to the very best advice, given by all the best journalists who had achieved the best sort of success in journalism; and then going away and doing the exact opposite. For what they all told me was that the secret of success in journalism was to study the particular journal and write what was suitable to it. And partly by accident and ignorance and partly through the real rabid certainties of youth, I cannot remember that I ever wrote any article that was at all suitable to any paper . . .

Autobiography, London 1936

'WHEN I CAME BACK TO FLEET STREET'

The first and last stanzas of a seven-stanza poem.

> When I came back to Fleet Street
> Through a sunset nook at night,
> And saw the old Green Dragon
> With the windows all alight,
> And hailed the old Green Dragon
> And the Cock I used to know,
> Where all good fellows were my friends

A little while ago . . .

. . . All that I loved and hated,
All that I shunned and knew,
Clears in broad battle lightning,
Where they, and I, and you,
Run high the barricade that breaks
The barriers of the street,
And shout to them that shrink within,
The Prisoners of the Fleet.

The Collected Poems of G. K. Chesterton, London 1933

QUALIFIED REMARKS

In the daily paper which had the largest circulation and the most influence . . . [a story] was committed to a gentleman known by what seemed to the non-journalistic world the singular name of Hibbs However. It had been affixed to him in jest in connexion with all the almost complicated caution with which all his public criticisms were qualified at every turn; so that everything came to depend upon the conjunctions; upon 'but' and 'yet' and 'though' and similar words. As his salary grew larger (for editors and proprietors like that sort of thing) . . . he grew more and more to value himself as a diplomatist; a man who always said the right thing. But he was not without his intellectual Nemesis; for at last he became so very diplomatic as to be darkly and densely unintelligible.

The Flying Inn, London 1914

CANT PHRASES

What I complain of . . . is the entirely mechanical use of certain cant phrases in current journalism. If a banker falls off an omnibus and is dragged along for a hundred yards by the left leg, the newspaper is now absolutely certain to head the paragraph 'Banker's Ordeal'. Now that is really a dead use of words, for the writer does not think *at all* about the original meaning of 'ordeal' as a deliberate test or trial.

The Illustrated London News, 8 January 1927

A FINE ROMANCE

Another word which goes along with 'ordeal' is 'romance'. It is always applied to the most unromantic marriage possible, as that of a pork millionaire with a mercenary chorus girl. It is always called 'Pork Millionaire's Romance'.

The Illustrated London News, 8 January 1927

THE EVENING PAPERS

. . . Evening papers are often more honest than morning papers, because they are written by ill-paid and hard-worked underlings in a great hurry; and there is no time for more timid people to correct them.

The Flying Inn, London 1914

HOW FREE?

. . . Unlike the press of Italy, the press of England is quite free. That is, editors are quite free to suppress any letters they choose, or black out any foreign news that does not happen to please them.

GK's Weekly, 6 March 1926

JOURNALESE

The journalistic version of events is 'made up'; not always in the sense of having been invented, but almost always in the sense of having been picked out and put together. Important things can be made insignificant, and insignificant things important. It resembles the similar modern process of flood-lighting, which is so called because it does not really cover everything like the flood. It picks out particular things with more than normal brightness and leaves other patches in more than usual blackness.

The Illustrated London News, 21 March 1936

VISIONARY

Word after word is struck dead with dullness, or rendered useless with misuse . . . I saw, the other day, with my own eyes, the following sentence printed in a leading article: 'Lord Rothermere has Vision'. I thought to myself: 'Bang! There goes another word! We shall never be able to use that seriously again.*

GK's Weekly, 13 September 1930

*Elsewhere, GKC wrote that the word 'dear' in 'Dear Sir', had also totally lost its meaning.

FOOTLOOSE

Some time ago . . . a paper blazed forth with a scare heading called 'The Menace of the Pedestrian'. It was one of the best jokes of recent times, for the best joke about the jokes of recent times is that nobody sees them, least of all the man who makes them.

GK's Weekly, 1 February 1930

THE LOCH NESS MONSTER

I need not say that such a Monster, whether or no he is an inhabitant of Loch Ness, is a very popular inhabitant of Fleet Street . . . [He] has helped many poor journalists to place paragraphs here and there. In the grand imagery of the Book of Job, he maketh the deep to boil like a pot; and has also been the occasion of a great deal of pot-boiling.

The Illustrated London News, 6 January 1934

ANON

The poet writing his name upon a score of little pages in the silence of his study, may or may not have an intellectual right to despise the journalist: but I greatly doubt whether he would not morally be the better if he saw the great lights burning on through darkness into dawn, and heard the roar of the printing wheels weaving the destinies of another day. Here at least is a school of labour and of some rough humility, the largest work ever published anonymously since the great Christian cathedrals.

'A Word for the Mere Journalist', *Darlington North Star*, 3 February 1902

HEADLINING

No journalist will complain of the journalistic necessity of occasionally changing a title, or especially abbreviating a title. If I choose to head an article 'An Enquiry into the Conditions of Mycenaean Civilization in the Heroic Epoch, with Special Reference to the Economic and Domestic Functions of Women Before and After the Conjectural Date of the Argive Expedition against Troy' – if, I say, I choose to give my article some snappy little title like that, I really have no right to com-

plain if (when I send it to the *Chicago Daily Scoop*) they alter
the title to 'How Helen Did the Housekeeping'.

The Illustrated London News, 19 January 1929

QUIZZES

On any [newspaper] page we may encounter the challenge –
'At what date did a dentist suffer death for his theological
opinions?' – or 'What deadly poison is a by-product of
crushed strawberries?' or 'What is the income of Mr Henry
Ford reckoned in ancient Greek drachmae?'

The Illustrated London News, 14 July 1928

TYPOS

Most journalists abound in jokes on the subject of misprints –
the fearful misprints that make nonsense and the far, far more
fearful misprints that make sense . . . I have had in my own
experience any number of the ordinary accidents, and have
had a great deal of amusement out of them. I have referred to
a very worthy Nonconformist minister as 'a distinguished
correspondent' and had the phrase printed as 'a distinguished
co-respondent'.

The Illustrated London News, 3 November 1928

UP TO THE MINUTE

The best information is very seldom the latest information.

The Illustrated London News, 14 July 1928

AN OPEN MIND

'Do you believe in curses?' asked Smaill curiously.

'I don't believe in anything; I'm a journalist,' answered the melancholy being – 'Boon, of the *Daily Wire* . . .'

'The Curse of the Golden Cross' (*The Father Brown Stories*)

A BAD PRESS

. . . I do feel very strongly about the frivolity and irresponsibility of the press. It seems impossible to exaggerate the evil that can be done by a corrupt and unscrupulous press. If drink directly ruins the family, it only indirectly ruins the nation. But bad journalism does directly ruin the nation, considered as a nation; it acts on the corporate national will and sways the common national decision. It may force a decision in a few hours that will be an incurable calamity for hundreds of years.

Fancies versus Fads, London 1923

ON THE OTHER HAND . . .

The very fact that we have seen a remark made a hundred times in the newspapers is normally a very good reason for considering seriously whether the opposite is not true.

The Illustrated London News, 8 September 1928

VICIOUS HOBBIES

Few realize how much of controversial war and tumult can be covered by an obscure hobby. The fighting spirit has almost taken refuge in hobbies as in holes and corners of the earth; and left the larger public fields singularly dull and flat and free from real debate. It might be imagined that the *Daily Wire* was a slashing paper and the *Review of Assyrian Excavation* was a mild and peaceful one. But in truth it is the other way. It is the popular paper that has become cold and conventional, and full of clichés used without any conviction. It is the scholarly paper that is full of fire and fanaticism and rivalry. Mr Herne could not contain himself when he thought of Professor Poole and his preposterous and monstrous suggestion about the Pre-Hittite sandal.

The Return of Don Quixote, London 1927

SUBURBAN NEIGHBOURS

Rustic villagers tell tales about their neighbours, true and false; but the curious culture of the modern suburb will believe anything it is told in the papers about the wickedness of the Pope, or the martyrdom of the King of the Cannibal Islands, and, in the excitement of these topics, never knows what is happening next door.

'The Man with Two Beards' (*The Father Brown Stories*)

DISGUSTED, TUNBRIDGE WELLS

. . . If an editor can only make people angry enough, they will write half his newspaper for him for nothing.

Heretics, London 1906

WHAT A BORE

I once had the pleasure of knowing a man who actually talked in private life after the manner of [newspapers]. His conversation consisted of fragmentary statements about height and weight and depth and time and population, and his conversation was a nightmare of dullness. During the shortest pause he would ask whether his interlocutors were aware of how many tons of rust were scraped every year off the Menai Bridge, and how many rival shops Mr Whiteley had bought up since he opened his business. The attitude of his acquaintance towards this inexhaustible entertainer varied . . . between indifference and terror. It was frightful to think of a man's brain being stocked with such inexpressibly profitless treasures. It was like visiting some imposing British Museum and finding its galleries filled with specimens of London mud, of common mortar, of broken walking-sticks and cheap tobacco.

The Defendant, London 1901

Years later GKC realized that the man had invented all his 'facts'.

BEHIND *THE TIMES*?

. . . Newspapers are never up to date. The men who write leading articles are always behind the times, because they are in a hurry. They are forced to fall back on their old-fashioned view of things; they have no time to fashion a new one.

George Bernard Shaw, London 1910

4
ART

MOOD AND MODE

The difficulty with art is that the artist is giving permanent expression to a passing mood. He may be, and generally is, also testifying to a truth that is permanently behind that mood. But he cannot make the mood itself as popular at one time as at another. He cannot be certain, at any given moment, of whether the mood is also the mode. Therefore, while the work may remain as a classic, it cannot remain, as does, for instance, a religion, continuing to produce its own types of saint or mystic generation after generation. That can only happen when the truths are crystallised into a creed, and are regarded by the people as truths and not as transitory moods.

The Illustrated London News, 22 December 1928

MODERN ART

At an exhibition of 'Post-Futurist' pictures, Lady Enid Brett's cousin Dorian Wimpole savages them.

All watchers for the Dawn will be deeply distressed to know that the Post-Futurist School of Painting received the full effects of [Dorian's] perverted wrath. In vain did Mr Leveson affirm from time to time 'People [are] always prejudiced against new ideas.' Vainly did Mr Hibbs say, at the proper intervals, 'After all, they said the same of Whistler.' Not by such decent formalities was the frenzy of Dorian to be appeased.

'That little Turk has more sense than you have,' he said; 'he passes it as a good wall-paper. I should say it was bad wall-paper; the sort of wall-paper that gives a sick man fever when he hasn't got it. But to call it pictures – you might as well call it seats for the Lord Mayor's Show.'

The Flying Inn, London 1914

MORE AT THE EXHIBITION

[Lord Ivywood's] cold eyes even shone; for though his pleasure was almost purely intellectual, it was utterly sincere.

'. . . I do trust the untried; I do follow the inexperienced,' he was saying quietly, with his fine inflections of voice. 'You say this is changing the very nature of Art. I want to change the very nature of Art. Everything lives by turning into something else. Exaggeration is growth.'

'But exaggeration of what?' demanded Dorian. 'I cannot see a trace of exaggeration in these pictures; because I cannot find a hint of what it is they want to exaggerate . . .'

The Flying Inn, London 1914

IMPUDENT

There is one very valid test by which we may separate genuine, if perverse and unbalanced, originality and revolt from mere impudent innovation and bluff. The man who really thinks he has an idea will always try to explain that idea. The charlatan who has no idea will always confine himself to explaining that it is much too subtle to be explained . . . Perhaps this distinction is most comically plain in the case of the thing called Art, and the people called Art Critics . . . Whistler and R. A. M. Stevenson . . . in the exposition of Velasquez . . . had something to say about the pictures; they knew it was unworthy of the pictures, but they said it. Now the eulogists of the latest artistic inanities (Cubism and Post-Impressionism and Mr Picasso) are eulogists and nothing else. They are not critics; least of all creative critics. They do not attempt to translate beauty into language; they merely tell you that it is untranslatable – that is, unutterable, indefinable, indescribable, impalpable, ineffable, and all the rest of it . . . They circulate a piece of paper on which Mr Picasso has had the misfortune to upset the ink and tried to dry it with his boots, and they seek to terrify democracy by the good old anti-democratic muddlements; that 'the public' does not understand these things.

Daily News, 9 December 1911

UNITY IN THE ARTS

The arts and crafts of man, from the beginning, have been arts and crafts of combination. They did unite the shelter of the roof and the dignity of the tower. They did unite the style of the orator with the decisions of the Forum. And they did unite the meaning of the words with the music of the tune . . . The union of sound and sense is a Marriage; and this is the age of Divorce. It cannot understand that divine paradox whereby two things become one and yet remain two.

The Illustrated London News, 25 August 1928

HANDS-ON ART APPRECIATION

Thousands of . . . visitors . . . study those endless lines of magnificent Pagan busts which are to be found in nearly all the

Italian galleries and museums, and admire them, and talk about them, and note them in their catalogues, and describe them in their diaries. But the way in which they affected Browning is described very suggestively in a passage in the letters of his wife. She describes herself as longing for her husband to write poems, beseeching him to write poems, but finding all her petitions useless because her husband was engaged all day in modelling busts in clay and breaking them as fast as he made them. This is Browning's interest in art, the interest in a living thing, the interest in a growing thing, the insatiable interest in how things are done. Everyone who knows his admirable poems on painting – 'Fra Lippo Lippi' and 'Andrea del Sarto' and 'Pictor ignotus' – will remember how fully they deal with technicalities, how they are concerned with canvas, with oil, with a mess of colours . . . These Browning poems do not merely deal with painting; they smell of paint. They are the works of a man to whom art is not what it is to so many of the non-professional lovers of art, a thing accomplished, a valley of bones; to him it is a field of crops continually growing in a busy and exciting silence. Browning was interested, like some scientific man, in the obstetrics of art . . . Browning could not merely talk art with artists – he could talk shop with them. Personally he may not have known enough about painting to be more than a fifth-rate painter . . . But there are . . . some things which a fifth-rate painter knows which a first-rate art critic does not know.

Robert Browning, London 1903

GKC's friend and sparring-partner, George Bernard Shaw, claimed that learning to play the piano, however badly, had made him a better music critic.

FASHIONS IN ART CRITICISM

The new artist may have been right about the new art; but he was very seldom right about the old art. A few generations later, a yet newer school of art will probably be worshipping the work which he despised . . . It is all to the good that the basilica should have its turn after the abbey, and the round Roman arch rise again in majesty after it has been apparently split asunder by the spear of the Gothic . . . But when this special enthusiasm leads a man to shutting his eyes, or putting out his tongue at Lincoln Cathedral or Leonardo da Vinci's pictures, I think we may be allowed to say that it has made him narrow, if not that it has made him blind.

The Illustrated London News, 18 August 1928

WILLIAM MORRIS

There seems to be something in the very nature of digging up a neglected masterpiece that renders a man irrationally irritated with things that the world has not neglected. He becomes an idolater about this image and an iconoclast about every other. William Morris was an artist and an art critic: but he could see nothing at all in Classical and Renaissance art. If anybody liked a building with a dome, he compared it to falling in love with a woman with a bald head.

The Illustrated London News, 18 August 1928

BRAWLING FOR ART

Morris was a man who wanted good wallpapers, not as a man wants a coin of the Emperor Constantine, which was the cloistered or abnormal way in which men had commonly devised such things: he wanted good wallpapers as a man wants beer. He clamoured for art: he brawled for it. He asserted the perfectly virile and ordinary character of the appetite for beauty.

G. F. Watts, London 1904

BACK TO THE DRAWING-BOARD

The most interesting and most supremely personal of all the elements in [Watts's] designs and draughtsmanship . . . is . . . his magnificent discovery of the artistic effect of the human back. The back is the most awful and mysterious thing in the universe; it is impossible to speak about it. It is the part of man that he knows nothing of; like an outlying province forgotten by an emperor. It is a common saying that anything may happen behind our backs: transcendentally considered, the thing has an eerie truth about it . . .

There is one possible exception to [Watts's] monopoly [of the back]. Two thousand years before, in the dark scriptures of a nomad people, it had been said that their prophet saw the immense Creator of all things, but only saw Him from behind. I do not know whether even Watts would dare to paint that.

G. F. Watts, London 1904

GKC specially praises two of Watts's paintings showing the human back – Eve Repentant *and* For He Had Great Possessions.

THE ARTIST'S MASK

Father Brown: '. . . We are talking about an artist; and for the enjoyment of the artist the mask must be to some extent moulded on the face. What he makes outside him must correspond to something inside him; he can only make his effects out of some of the materials of his soul.'

'The Curse of the Golden Cross' (*The Father Brown Stories*)

ARTISTIC INTEGRITY

'It isn't defending a man to say he is a genius,' said Father Brown. 'Far from it. And it is simply a psychological fact that an artist will betray himself by some sort of sincerity. Leonardo da Vinci cannot draw as if he couldn't draw. Even if he tried, it will always be a strong parody of a weak thing.'

'The Curse of the Golden Cross' (*The Father Brown Stories*)

5

ARCHITECTURE

A CATHOLIC TASTE

The classical fountains in Rome are not necessarily bad because the pointed shrines in Normandy are good . . . We may well admit that, even when we are illuminated with all the windows of Chartres, even when we are rejoicing in some glorious Gothic lantern of flamboyant glass, we are in a sense living in glass houses and should not throw stones.

The Illustrated London News, 12 March 1927

HUG A HOODIE

. . . 'Do you know,' [Herne] added abruptly and in a lowered voice, 'there's something very satisfying about wearing a hood . . . something symbolical. I don't wonder they corrupted the name of the great medieval hero into Robin Hood.'

. . . 'What do you mean,' [Olive] said, 'by saying a hood is symbolical?'

'Have you never looked through an archway', asked Herne, 'and seen the landscape beyond as bright as a lost paradise? That is because there is a frame to the picture . . . You are cut off from something and allowed to look at something. When will people understand that the world is a window and not a blank infinity; a window in a wall of infinite nothing? When I wear this hood I carry my window with me. I say to myself – this is the world that Francis of Assisi saw and loved because it was limited. The hood has the very shape of a Gothic window.'

The Return of Don Quixote, London 1927

MARBLE ARCH

The Marble Arch . . . in its new insular position, with traffic turning dizzily all about it, struck me as a placid monstrosity. What could be wilder than to have a huge arched gateway, with people going everywhere except under it? If I took down my front door and stood it up all by itself in the middle of my back garden, my village neighbours (in their simplicity) would probably stare. Yet the Marble Arch is now precisely that; an elaborate entrance and the only place by which no one can enter.

'The Anarchist', *Alarms and Discursions*, London 1911

NOT BATS ABOUT THE BELFRY

I have been standing where everybody else has stood, opposite the Belfry Tower of Bruges, and thinking, as every one has thought (though not, perhaps, said), that it is built in defiance of all decencies of architecture. It is made in deliberate disproportion to achieve the one startling effect of height. It is a church on stilts. But this sort of sublime deformity is characteristic of the whole fancy and energy of these Flemish cities. Flanders has the flattest and most prosaic of landscapes, but the most violent and extravagant of buildings. Here Nature is tame; it is civilization that is untamable . . . All Christian temples worth talking about have gargoyles; but Bruges' Belfry is a gargoyle.

Tremendous Trifles, London 1909

CHRIST AND THE GOTHIC

Christ prophesied the whole of Gothic architecture in that hour when nervous and respectable people (such people as now object to barrel organs) objected to the shouting of the gutter-snipes of Jerusalem. He said, 'If these were silent, the very stones would cry out.' Under the impulse of His spirit arose like a clamorous chorus the façades of the medieval cathedrals, thronged with shouting faces and open mouths.

Orthodoxy, London 1909

POINTED REMARK

[Olive Ashley:] 'I don't want to look down at all. That's why I like all this old Gothic painting and building; in Gothic all the lines go upwards, right up to the very spire that points to heaven.'

'It's rude to point,' said Murrel, 'and I think they might have given us credit for noticing the sky.'

The Return of Don Quixote, London 1927

THE GOTHIC REVIVAL

The real trouble has been that even those who admired Gothic most could not revive the part of it that was most admirable. The most wonderful thing about Gothic was the spontaneous individual craftsmanship, especially in its sanctification of the grotesque. But there was nothing specially spontaneous, there was nothing specially individual, there was certainly nothing grotesque, about the pallid and pointed church architecture that began with the Victorian high churchmen and is now the pattern of every Wesleyan or Congregationalist chapel in Surbiton or Streatham.

The Illustrated London News, 12 March 1927

SCAFFOLDING

A house was being built near GKC's in the country.

It is odd that the skeleton of a house is cheerful when the skeleton of a man is mournful, since we only see it after the man is destroyed . . . There is something strangely primary and poetic about this sight of the scaffolding and main lines of a human building; it is a pity there is no scaffolding round a human baby.

'The Wings of Stone', *Alarms and Discursions*, London 1911

DOWN THE TUBE

There is one of the modern works of engineering that gives one something of this nameless fear of the exaggerations of an underworld; and that is the curious curved architecture of the underground railway, commonly called the Twopenny Tube. Those squat archways, without any up-right line or pillar, look as if they had been tunnelled by huge worms who have never learnt to lift their heads. It is the very underground palace of the Serpent . . .

What's Wrong with the World, London 1910

MODERN ARCHITECTURE

The new scientific architecture can be perfected to a point of ghastly and demoniac ugliness towards which the dark fancies of our savage fathers would grope in vain.

The Illustrated London News, 17 March 1928

6

HISTORY

including the history of GKC's own times

PARCELLING UP HISTORY

Nothing can be imagined more idle, in a general way, than talking about a century as if it were some kind of animal with a head and tail, instead of an arbitrary length cut from an unending scroll. Nor is it less erroneous to assume that even if a period be definitely vital or disturbing, art must be a mirror of it; the greatest political storm flutters only a fringe of humanity; poets, like bricklayers, work on through a century of wars, and Bewick's birds, to take an instance, have the air of persons unaffected by the French Revolution.

G. F. Watts, London 1904

STONEHENGE

. . . To a person really capable of feeling the poetry of Stonehenge it is almost a secondary matter whether he sees Stonehenge at all. The vast void roll of the empty land towards Salisbury, the grey tablelands like primeval altars, the trailing rain-clouds, the vapour of primeval sacrifices, would all tell him of a very ancient and very lonely Britain. It would not spoil his Druidic mood if he missed Stonehenge. But it does spoil his mood to find Stonehenge – surrounded by a brand-new fence of barbed wire, with a policeman and a little shop selling picture post-cards.

Now if you protest against this, educated people will instantly answer you: 'Oh, it was done to prevent the vulgar trippers who chip stones and carve names and spoil the look of Stonehenge.' It does not seem to occur to them that barbed wire and a policeman rather spoil the look of Stonehenge.

Daily News, 15 June 1912

KING ARTHUR

When Tennyson says that King Arthur 'drew all the petty princedoms under him', and 'made a realm and ruled', his grave Royalism is quite modern . . . But that older verse:

> When good King Arthur ruled this land
> He was a goodly King –
> He stole three pecks of barley-meal
> To make a bag-pudding,

is far more Arthurian than anything in *The Idylls of the King*.

Daily News, 30 December 1911

FAERIE QUEENE

I have admired Queen Elizabeth in my boyhood and disliked her in my manhood, and I am now strongly inclined to believe that both the good Elizabeth and the bad Elizabeth are legends.

The Illustrated London News, 7 April 1928

GETTING ELIZABETH WRONG

To paint a portrait of Queen Elizabeth as a prophetic lioness of Protestantism, upholding the Huguenots out of mere love of the Holy Scriptures, and brandishing a Bible to cow all the Papists of the world, is not a process of portraiture true but incomplete; it is simply completely untrue. It is contradicted by every fact in Elizabeth's history, from her continuous invalidism or ill-health to her continuous intrigues about marrying Catholic princes.

The Illustrated London News, 14 February 1931

WILLIAM CECIL

I fancy William Cecil cared more for his country seat than for his country, but I think it probable that he did care for his country.

GK's Weekly, 3 January 1935

CHARLES I THE SOCIALIST

. . . Charles I might very well belong to the Labour Party rather than the Liberal Party or the Conservative Party. Those who do not understand this do not understand what Charles I did or even what Labour is supposed to do. For instance, he would certainly have been in favour of the Nationalization of Mines. Indeed, we may say that he was in favour of the Nationalization of Mines. One of the most determining questions on which he differed from his Parliamentary aristocracy was his insistence that metals and minerals ought not to be private property, but ought to belong to the Crown – or, in other words, the State. Some of us think that on this point Charles I was quite right.

The Illustrated London News, 9 February 1927

OLIVER CROMWELL

[Murrel says:] 'I should say that the one place where we never have wanted a strong man is England. I can only remember one person who went into the profession, poor old Cromwell; and the consequence was that we dug him up to hang him after he was dead and went mad with joy for a month because the throne was going back to a weak man – or one we thought was a weak man. These high-handed ways don't suit us a bit, either revolutionary or reactionary.'

The Return of Don Quixote, London 1927

ORANGES AND CHERRIES

The English aristocrats of the Revolution did not nibble at James II, like a cherry; they dropped him like a hot potato. Neither did they nibble at William of Orange like a cherry; they swallowed him like a pill.

The Illustrated London News, 23 July 1910

LOUIS XIV

It is much nearer the truth to compare him to a sun-god than to compare him to a pompous dancing-master, in the manner of the narrow national bigotry of Macaulay.

The Illustrated London News, 5 September 1931

RIGHT SIDE UP?

. . . As history is taught, nearly everybody assumes that in all important past conflicts, it was the right side that won.

Everybody assumes it; and nobody knows that he assumes it. The man has simply never seriously entertained the other notion. Say to him that we should now all of us be better off if Charles Edward and the Jacobites had captured London instead of falling back from Derby, and he will laugh . . . I am not discussing whether it was right as a theory; I am only noting that it is never allowed to occur to anybody as a thought.

The Thing, New York 1930

PRESS ON REGARDLESS

While all the English were sneering at the wild Jacobin, Bonaparte, for introducing the new notion of a conscript army, they were having a conscript Navy of their own on the sly. That, I fear, is the historical truth about the press gang.

The Illustrated London News, 4 October 1913

FAG-ENDS

It is very unfortunate that we so often know a thing that is past only by its tail end. We remember yesterday only by its sunsets. There are many instances. One is Napoleon. We always think of him as a fat old despot, ruling Europe with a ruthless military machine. But that, as Lord Rosebery would say, was only 'The Last Phase'; or at least the last but one. During the strongest and most startling part of his career, the time that made him immortal, Napoleon was a sort of boy, and not a bad sort of boy either . . .

'A Drama of Dolls', *Alarms and Discursions*, London 1911

THE SICK MAN OF EUROPE?

Everybody knows that one of the last Tsars said that the Turk was a very sick man, and that if he died soon we should have the problem of administering his property; especially the delicate task of administering it to ourselves. Since then, as very often happens, the sick man has conspicuously survived the strong man.

The Illustrated London News, 11 August 1928

YOUNG TURKS

What the Young Turks did was to take what was in many ways a broad religion and narrow it into a nation. There was no such thing as a European nation of Turkey, any more than there is any such thing as a European nation of Tibet . . . The thing that bound [the Turks] together in battle or in pilgrimage, the thing that they all understood and the thing that made them count in the affairs of their fellow men, was a loyalty to the Sultan simply as the head of the world of Islam . . .

The Illustrated London News, 11 August 1928

THE IRISH FAMINE

The Irish Famine was more than an earthquake; it was an explosion . . . As an explosion scatters the arms and legs of a single man, so this catastrophe scattered the separated parts of a single people . . . The ruin of Ireland simply strewed the whole earth with the enemies of England.

The Illustrated London News, 4 April 1936

JOHN BULL'S OTHER ISLAND

I should once have said that England had not governed Ireland well, because she had not sympathetically understood a different and subtle national soul. Now I should say that England has not governed Ireland well because England has never tried.

The Illustrated London News, 25 October 1913

SOMETHING PERSONAL

The great duel between Gladstone and Disraeli . . . was certainly personal as well as political.

The Illustrated London News, 26 September 1931

AN AGE ECLIPSED

It will appear to many a somewhat grotesque matter to talk about a period in which most of us were born and which has only been dead a year or two, as if it were a primal Baylonian empire of which only a few columns are left crumbling in the desert. And yet such is, in spirit, the fact. There is no more remarkable psychological element in history than the way in which a period can suddenly become unintelligible. To the early Victorian period we have in a moment lost the key; the Crystal Palace is the temple of a forgotten creed. The thing always happens sharply: a whisper runs through the salons, Mr Max Beerbohm waves a wand and a whole generation of great men and great achievement suddenly looks mildewed and unmeaning.

G. F. Watts, London 1904

COUP D'ÉTAT

I believe I am the only man alive who is ready to utter a eulogy on Louis Napoleon, commonly called Napoleon the Third. He figures as the villain of the Victorian age, because he had discovered what all that age had denied; the falsehood of the all-sufficiency of Parliaments.

GK's Weekly, 5 June 1926

THE BOER WAR

Mr Belloc and myself . . . were much more concerned to say that the Boers were right to fight than that the British were wrong to fight.

GK's Weekly, 11 April 1931

KAISER BILL AN AESTHETE

It has always struck me that the German Emperor is a person whose real character would repay study. I need hardly say that I shall never see him closely enough to study it. But I am sure there is no truth in either of the two ordinary versions of him: the first which apparently represents him as a crusader permanently in the moonlight; and the second, which represents him as a mountebank permanently in the limelight. The latter version may be seen in English caricatures, the former in German statues – which are funnier than English caricatures. A man is not necessarily unwise because he is fond of changing his clothes; the hundred uniforms may be merely the artistic temperament . . . The Germans have always expected their Kings to be aesthetes. Even the mad King of Bavaria was not so mad – for Bavaria – as he would have been for Buckingham Palace. Much of the dislike felt in England for the Prince

Consort arose from our feeling something priggish in what his countrymen would think merely princely – the patronage of art and education.

The Illustrated London News, 13 December 1913

THE FIRST WORLD WAR

I do not agree with Mr H. G. Wells . . . that the Great War was a war that settled nothing, any more than I agreed with Mr H. G. Wells that it was the war that would end war. It was quite enough for me, from the first, that it was the war that would end Prussian prestige; and it did.

The Illustrated London News, 14 April 1928

JOSEPH CHAMBERLAIN

Mr Chamberlain . . . constantly eludes or vanquishes his opponents because his real powers and deficiencies are quite different from those with which he is credited, both by friends and foes. His friends depict him as a strenuous man of action; his opponents depict him as a coarse man of business; when, as a fact, he is neither one nor the other, but an admirable romantic orator and romantic actor. He has one power which is the soul of melodrama – the power of pretending, even when backed by a huge majority, that he has his back to the wall . . . He talks foolishly and yet very finely about his own city [Birmingham] that has never deserted him. He wears a flaming and fantastic flower, like a decadent minor poet.* As for his bluffness and toughness and appeals to common sense, all that is, of course, simply the first trick of rhetoric. He fronts his audiences with the venerable affectation of Mark Antony – 'I am no orator, as Brutus is; but as you know me all, a plain blunt man.'

It is the whole difference between the aim of the orator and the aim of any other artist, such as the poet or the sculptor. The aim of the sculptor is to convince us that he is a sculptor; the aim of the orator is to convince us that he is not an orator.

Heretics, London 1906

*Joseph Chamberlain was famous for sporting an orchid in his buttonhole. One cartoon showed him answering 'an orchid question'. Chamberlain (1836–1914), Mayor of Birmingham in the 1870s, was elected MP for the city in 1876, and rose to be Colonial Secretary. A. J. P. Taylor considered him 'the best prime minister we never had'.

Illustration 9: Caricature of Joseph Chamberlain by Harry Furniss.

LEAGUE OF NATIONS

A League of Nations really stands or falls with the truth of its title. If it is really a League of Nations it may really be a noble thing; but, as presented by some people, it is rather a League for the Abolition of Nations. It is not a scheme to guarantee the independence of States, but at best to guarantee their safety if they will sacrifice their independence.

The Illustrated London News, 13 July 1918

A PLAGUE ON BOTH YOUR HOUSES

I am myself in a certain sense detached touching the Bolshevist controversy, with all the serene detachment of detestation. For I detest both the capitalism it denounces and the communism it decrees.

The Illustrated London News, 4 October 1919

CAN GERMANY BE TRUSTED?

There is one aspect of all the talk about the trial of the Kaiser which seems to be strangely neglected . . . It may be put shortly by saying that to deal with him as the devil of Germany does definitely imply that the devil has been cast out . . .

Now it is a far more practical problem for the future whether we can trust what is now the German republic than whether we can trust one particular man who is no longer the German Emperor.

The Illustrated London News, 19 July 1919

CHURCHILL AND BONAR LAW

. . . I saw the other day, of all extraordinary things in the world, that Mr Winston Churchill had accused Mr Bonar Law of wishing to go back to the Middle Ages. This is undoubtedly, in my opinion, a very high compliment; but I cannot imagine anyone who could possibly deserve the compliment less than Mr Bonar Law. He is the very embodiment of everything that only began when the Middle Ages ended: the Colonial type, the commercial test, the Scotch Puritan tradition.

The Illustrated London News, 18 November 1922

ALTERNATIVE HISTORY

The test of a man's culture and liberality is his attitude towards the things that never happened . . . By the things that never happened, I mean the things that nearly happened . . . I mean the alternative history of England or France or Rome . . . One of the things that nearly happened [in the Middle Ages] was a single, solid United Kingdom of Anglo-France . . . [but] at the moment the two nations are rather less like one nation than any two nations of the world . . . I cannot think [the world] has ever gone *steadily* anywhere.

The Illustrated London News, 27 April 1929

THE ABYSSINIAN WOUND

I detest the Abyssinian adventure; I would have given almost anything to prevent it happening at all; for I see clearly that it will inflict a wound not merely on Africa, but on Europe.

GK's Weekly, 9 January 1936

7

HISTORIANS

HISTORIOGRAPHY

I wonder nobody has ever written a History of the Histories of England. The historians would themselves be characters in a very entertaining play. Summaries of their treatment of the same subject would have something of the unexpected variety of the versions of the same story in Browning's experiment of *The Ring and the Book*. Anyhow, the historians would be very vivid characters; some of them, to tell the truth, rather comic characters.

'About Historians', *As I Was Saying*, London 1936

AUTRES TEMPS, AUTRES MOEURS?

The historian has a habit of saying of people in the past: 'I think they may well be considered worthy of praise, allowing for the ideas of their times.' There will never be really good history until the historian says, 'I think they were worthy of praise, allowing for the ideas of *my* time.' The star-gazing mathematician, when he allows for the personal equation, allows for it in his own person, not in some other person living down the road . . .

The Illustrated London News, 15 August 1925

UNFATHOMABLE WELLS

Why dreams are different from daylight, why dead things are different from live things, why [a man] is different from others, why beauty makes us restless and even love is a spring of quarrels, why we cannot so fit into our environment as to forget it and ourselves; all these things are felt vaguely by children on long empty afternoons; or by primitive poets writing the epics and legends of the morning of the world. And all legends, however barbaric, are filled with the wind of all this wider questioning. They all refer back to these ancient unfathomable wells which go down deeper than the reason into the very roots of the world, but contain the springs that refresh the reason and keep it active for ever. The object of the rationalist historian is to choke up those wells. He puts in a sort of plug, like a stupid plumber, to stop the flowing of the fountain of youth.

The Illustrated London News, 6 August 1932

LORD MACAULAY

I read Macaulay when I was a boy and believed him, because I was a boy. I might almost say because he was a boy. For the best and heartiest thing about Macaulay was that he lived and died a boy: full of conviction, ignorant of life; cocksure and confident of the future. And in Macaulay's Essays will be found all that theory of the succession of things more and more 'advanced' which the artistic schools still repeat, still scornfully hurl against each other, and still meekly inherit from each other.

The Illustrated London News, 6 October 1928

GREAT MEN VERSUS MOVEMENTS

Thomas Carlyle was a great man who would hear of nothing but great men. Mr H. G. Wells is a great man who will hear of nothing but great mobs and great movements. Cromwell was a great man; but it is obvious that in the Puritan revolt he had a great opportunity. But Carlyle always wrote as if Cromwell would have been exactly the same without the Ironsides. And Mr Wells always wrote as if the Grand Army would have been exactly the same without Napoleon.

The Illustrated London News, 12 February 1927

8

SCIENCE

APPLIED SCIENCE

There is one aspect of modern science and machinery that nobody has noticed. It is quite new, and it is enormously important. It is this: that the very fact of using new methods makes it easier to fall back on old morals, especially if they are very immoral morals. If we seem to be putting new tools to new uses, we do not notice that the new uses are old abuses. I remember reading in cold print in a current newspaper a report, calmly describing how an obstinately silent tramp had been given shocks with an electric battery to make him speak. I read it with horror; but the horror did not seem to be general. Now, if the newspaper had told us that the police had taken the tramp to the Tower, and given him even the tiniest turn of the thumbscrew or a single moment's experience of the rack, everybody in England would have been shocked and all the humanitarians would have been shrieking. Yet the thing was exactly the same: it was simply forcing speech by inflicting pain, or threatening to inflict it . . . Because it was a modern instrument of science, men could hardly realise that it was being used as an ancient instrument of torture.

The Illustrated London News, 4 February 1928

GKC goes on to suggest that the Government feels it can censor wire-less broadcasting, in a way it would not be able to censor the press.

ALL-ELECTRIC

I am informed that there is an elaborately electrified house on view: a house in which the householder can be completely electrified, or possibly electro-plated, or perhaps eventually electrocuted . . . Indeed, when I heard a lecturer a little while ago explain at some length (with the assistance of lantern-slides) the complicated but complete apparatus of such a domestic system, I ventured to ask whereabouts in the electric house they had fitted up the electric chair.

The Illustrated London News, 17 March 1928

A CHAIR FOR UNWELCOME GUESTS

If I had a nice, neat, comfortable electric chair fitted up in my house . . . I could quietly and quickly make a clearance of a great many . . . social difficulties. It would be easy to receive a particular guest with gestures of hospitality; to wave him to a special seat with a special earnestness; to see him settled comfortably in it; and then to press a button with a smile and a sigh of relief.

The Illustrated London News, 17 March 1928

SCIENCE AND RELIGION

As for science and religion, the known and admitted facts are few and plain enough. All that the parsons say is unproved. All that the doctors say is disproved. That's the only difference between science and religion there's ever been, or will be.

Manalive, 1915

9

ENGLAND AND
THE ENGLISH

'THE SECRET PEOPLE'

The first and last stanzas of a six-stanza poem.

Smile at us, pass us; but do not quite forget.
For we are the people of England, that never have
    spoken yet.
There is many a fat farmer that drinks less cheerfully,
There is many a free French peasant who is richer
    and sadder than we.
There are no folk in the whole world so helpless or so wise,
There is hunger in our bellies, there is laughter in our eyes;
You laugh at us and love us, both mugs and eyes are wet:
Only you do not know us. For we have not spoken yet. . .

. . . We hear men speaking for us of new laws strong
    and sweet,
Yet is there no man speaketh as we speak in the street.
It may be we shall rise the last as Frenchmen rose the first,
Our wrath come after Russia's wrath and our wrath
    be the worst.
It may be we are meant to mark with our riot and our rest
God's scorn for all men governing.
It may be beer is best.
But we are the people of England; and we have not
    spoken yet.
Smile at us, pay us, pass us.
But do not quite forget.

The Collected Poems of G. K. Chesterton, London 1933

ENGLISH PHLEGM

Perhaps the real meaning of St George and the dragon is that an evil has to be about as big and ugly as a dragon before an Englishman even knows it is there.

GK's Weekly, St George's Day, 23 April 1927

ENGLISH PSYCHOLOGY

What is curious about the English psychology is this: that it has this purely artistic appetite and then persuades itself that it is practical.

The Illustrated London News, 26 March 1927

THE ROMANTIC ENGLISH

We have as a nation got our ideas out of novels and plays and poetic romances, much more than out of economic text-books or even commercial ledgers.

The Illustrated London News, 26 March 1927

THE ENGLISH SENSE OF HUMOUR

What pikes and shillelahs were to the Irish populace, what guns and barricades were to the French populace, that chaff is to the English populace. It is their weapon, the use of which they really understand. It is the one way in which they can make a rich man feel uncomfortable, and they use it justifiably for all it is worth.

Introduction to Dickens's *Great Expectations*, London 1907

WHY ENGLISH ROADS TWIST ABOUT

The beginning of a long poem.

> Some say that Guy of Warwick,
> The man that killed the Cow
> And brake the mighty Boar alive
> Beyond the Bridge at Slough;
> Went up against a Loathly Worm
> That wasted all the Downs,
> And so the roads they twist and squirm
> (If I may be allowed the term)
> From the writhing of the striken Worm
> That died in seven towns . . .

'The Secret People', *The Flying Inn*, London 1914

EUROPEAN COMMUNITY

There is one good test and one only of whether a man has travelled to any profit in Europe. An Englishman is, as such, a European, and as he approaches the central splendours of Europe he ought to feel that he is coming home. If he does not feel at home he had much better have stopped at home . . . Your visit to Europe is useless unless it gives you the sense of an exile returning.

Introduction to Dickens's *A Tale of Two Cities*, London 1909

10

LONDON

RIVER OF FIRE

He walked on the Embankment once under a dark red sunset. The red river reflected the red sky, and they both reflected his anger. The sky, indeed, was so swarthy, and the light on the river relatively so lurid, that the water almost seemed of fiercer flame than the sunset it mirrored. It looked like a stream of literal fire winding under the vast caverns of a subterranean country.

The Man Who Was Thursday, London 1908

NORTH LONDON

The vast blank space of North London was flying by; the very pace gave us a sense of its immensity and its meanness. It was, as it were, a base infinitude, a squalid eternity, and we felt the real horror of the poor parts of London, the horror that is so totally missed and misrepresented by the sensational novelists who depict it as being a matter of narrow streets, filthy houses, criminals and maniacs, and dens of vice. In a narrow street, in a den of vice, you do not expect civilization, you do not expect order. But the horror of this was the fact that there was civilization, that there was order, but that civilization only showed its morbidity, and order only its monotony. No one would say in going through a criminal slum, 'I see no statues. I notice no cathedrals.' But here there were public buildings;

only they were mostly lunatic asylums. Here there were statues; only they were mostly statues of railway engineers and philanthropists – two dingy classes of people united by their common contempt for the people. Here there were churches; only they were the churches of dim and erratic sects, Agapemonites or Irvingites. Here, above all, there were broad roads and vast crossings and tramway lines and hospitals and all the real marks of civilization. But though one never knew, in one sense, what one would see next, there was one thing we knew we should not see – anything really great, central, of the first class, anything that humanity had adored.

The Club of Queer Trades, London 1905

THE GROVE OF THE EVANGELIST

'I cannot think', [said the King,] 'why people should think the names of places in the country more poetical than those in London. Shallow romanticists go away in trains and stop in places called Hugmy-in-the-Hole, or Bumps-on-the-Puddle. And all the time they could, if they liked, go and live at a place with the dim, divine name of St John's Wood. I have never been to St John's Wood. I dare not. I should be afraid of the innumerable night of fir trees, afraid to come upon a blood-red cup and the beating of the wings of the Eagle . . .'

The Napoleon of Notting Hill, London 1904

BEDFORD PARK

The suburb of Saffron Park lay on the sunset side of London, as red and ragged as a cloud of sunset. It was built of a bright brick throughout; its skyline was fantastic, and even its ground plan was wild. It had been the outburst of a speculative builder, faintly tinged with art, who called its architecture sometimes Elizabethan and sometimes Queen Anne, apparently under the impression that the two sovereigns were identical.★

The Man Who Was Thursday, London 1908

★As we have seen, Bedford Park (here thinly disguised as 'Saffron Park') was where GKC met his future wife, Frances Blogg. It was (and is) an estate of arty villas, some of them designed by Norman Shaw, near Turnham Green Underground station.

11
CLASS

ENGLAND'S CUNNING ARISTOS

. . . It was the fashion in the Victorian times, to say that England was represented by its Great Middle Class and not by its aristocracy. That was the artfulness of its aristocracy. Never did a governing class govern so completely, by saying it did not govern at all.

The Illustrated London News, 15 March 1930

NOBLESSE DOESN'T ALWAYS *OBLIGE*

Father Brown: 'The legal witnesses . . . are Lady Miriam and her friend, Miss Talbot. I suppose you feel sure *they* are all right?'

'Lady Miriam?' said Jarvis in surprise. 'Oh, yes . . . I suppose you mean that she looks a queer sort of vamp. But you've no notion what even the ladies of the best families are looking like nowadays . . .'

'The Actor and the Alibi' (*The Father Brown Stories*)

LAUGHING STOCK

. . . We in Europe never really and at the root of our souls took aristocracy seriously . . . The great and obvious merit of the English aristocracy is that nobody could possibly take it seriously.

Orthodoxy, London 1909

BLUE BLOODY

. . . Aristocrats exhibit less of the romance of pedigree than any other people in the world. For since it is their principle to marry only within their own class and mode of life, there is no opportunity in their case for any of the more interesting studies in heredity; they exhibit almost the unbroken uniformity of the lower animals. It is in the middle classes that we find the poetry of genealogy; it is the suburban grocer standing at his shop door whom some wild dash of Eastern or Celtic blood may drive suddenly to a whole holiday or a crime.

Robert Browning, London 1903

VEGGIES

'You see,' [Pump] said to his friend the Captain, 'eating vegetables isn't half bad, so long as you know what vegetables there are and eat all of them that you can. But . . . it goes wrong among the gentry . . . They've never had to eat a carrot or a potato because it was all there was in the house; so they've never learnt how to be really hungry for carrots, as that donkey might be.'

The Flying Inn, London 1914

'THE ARISTOCRAT'

The Devil is a gentleman, and asks you down to stay
At his little place at What'sitsname (it isn't far away.)
They say the sport is splendid; there is always
  something new,
And fairy scenes, and fearful feats that none but he
  can do;
He can shoot the feathered cherubs if they fly on
  the estate,
Or fish for Father Neptune with the mermaids for a bait;
He sealed amid the staggering stars that precipice, the sky,
And blew his trumpet above heaven, and got by mastery
The starry crown of God Himself, and shoved it on
  the shelf;
But the Devil is a gentleman, and doesn't brag himself.

O blind your eyes and break your heart and hack
  your hand away,
And lose your love and shave your head; but do not
  go to stay
At the little place in What'sitsname where folks are
  rich and clever;
The golden and the goodly house, where things grow
  worse for ever;
There are things you need not know of, though you live
  and die in vain,
There are souls more sick of pleasure than you are
  sick of pain;
There is a game of April Fool that's played behind
  its door,
Where the fool remains for ever and the April comes
  no more,
Where the splendour of the daylight grows drearier
  than the dark,

And life droops like a vulture that once was such a lark:
And that is the Blue Devil that once was the Blue Bird;
For the Devil is a gentleman, and doesn't keep his word.

'The Aristocrat'

SNOB STORIES

A barbarian worshipping Odin was not personally ashamed
that he was not one of the gods in Asgard. But a modern snob,
worshipping aristocracy, really is ashamed that he is not one of
the aristocrats. That is the very vital difference between
submission to superstition and submission to snobbery.

The Illustrated London News, 23 August 1913

AGENT NOT A GENT

Mr Bullrose was not a nice man. The agent on that sort of
estate hardly ever is a nice man. The landlord often is; and
even Lord Ivywood had an arctic magnanimity of his own,
which made most people want, if possible, to see him personally. But Mr Bullrose was petty. Every really practical tyrant
must be petty.

The Flying Inn, London 1914

A PIG IN A PEW

'. . . The Ivywoods were always cranky. It's only fair to him
to remember his grandfather . . . I never was hard on the case
myself; we all have our little ways. I shouldn't like it done to
my pig; but I don't see why a man shouldn't have his own pig

in his own pew with him if he likes it. It wasn't a free seat. It was the family pew.'

The Flying Inn, London 1914

MATCHING COATS

Few persons receiving a coat of arms would not be slightly dashed in their delight on learning that the same blazonry had been given to everybody in the same town at the same moment . . . But this could be done; this would really be what is called Levelling Up.

GK's Weekly, 9 June 1928

HERALDIC DEVICES

If a man were to blazon a bacillus on his shield, it would would not be instantly recognized, like a lion or a leopard . . . If a man were to wave a flag decorated with three microbes on a chevron, it would not have the inspiring effect of the old French flag decorated with lilies, or even of the yet older Frankish flag said to have been decorated with toads.

The Illustrated London News, 25 July 1931

SERVES THEM RIGHT

. . . The secret of aristocracy is hidden even from aristocrats. Servants, butlers, footmen, are the high priests who have the real dispensation; and even gentlemen are afraid of them. Dickens was never more right than when he made the new people, the Veneerings, employ a butler who despised not only them but all their guests and acquaintances.

Introduction to Dickens's *Our Mutual Friend*, London 1908

In this passage GKC anticipates P. G. Wodehouse's Jeeves; and Hilaire Belloc wrote, in 'Lord Lundy' (1907) these lines:

> *In my opinion, Butlers ought*
> *To know their place, and not to play*
> *The Old Retainer night and day.*

THE CASTE SYSTEM

The Caste System of India . . . seems to me to be a tyranny; and the worst sort of tyranny, which is not conducted by a tyrant, but by an aristocracy; but it is not a hypocrisy. It is not even that more confused and unconscious sort of hypocrisy that we call humbug. It is not confused at all; its very cruelty is in its clarity. You cannot play about with the idea of a Brahmin as you can with the idea of a Gentleman. You cannot pretend that Pariahs were made Pariahs entirely as a compliment to them, and in the interests of True Democracy.

'On the Simplicity of Asia', *All I Survey*, London 1933

PEARLS BEFORE SWINE

The snobbishness of bad literature . . . is not servile; but the snobbishness of good literature is servile. The old–fashioned halfpenny romance where the duchesses sparkled with diamonds was not servile; but the new romance where they sparkle with epigrams is servile. For in thus attributing a special and startling degree of intellect and conversational or controversial power to the upper classes, we are attributing something which is not especially their virtue or even especially their aim.

Heretics, London 1906

CALL A SPADE A SPADE

[Braintree asks Herne:] 'What do you mean exactly by saying that this old society of yours was sane?'

'I mean that the old society was truthful and that you are in a tangle of lies,' answered Herne. 'I don't mean that it was perfect or painless. I mean that it called pain and imperfection by their names. You talk about despots and vassals and all the rest; well, you also have coercion and inequality; but you dare not call anything by its own Christian name. You defend every single thing by saying it is something else. You have a King and then explain that he is not allowed to be a King. You have a House of Lords and say it is the same as a House of Commons. When you do want to flatter a workman or a peasant you say he is a true gentleman; which is like saying he is a veritable viscount. When you want to flatter the gentleman you say he does not use his own title . . . You have teachers who refuse doctrine, which only means teaching; and doctors of divinity disavowing anything divine. It is all false and cowardly and shamefully full of shame. Everything is prolonging its existence by denying that it exists.'

The Return of Don Quixote, London 1927

SIGN-OFFS

When the Pope in an Encyclical calls himself your father, it is a matter of faith or of doubt. But when the Duke of Devonshire in a letter calls himself yours obediently, you know that he means the opposite of what he says.

'A Dead Poet', *All Things Considered*, London 1908

WELL OCCUPIED

There is a nursery jingle existing, I believe, in many forms and describing the chief types of trades; the version of my own childhood was: 'Tinker, tailor, soldier, sailor, gentleman, pothecary, ploughboy, thief.'* It is not to be offered as a strictly exhaustive summary of the *quicquid agunt homines*, omitting as it does all mention of astrologers, ostrich-farmers, organists, professional monstrosities, and other happy walks of life, nor is it indeed strictly logical in its categories, some of which may be supposed to overlap. Thus, a man might be a sailor and a thief, like Blackbeard or Captain Kidd; or a gentleman and an apothecary, like the father of Arthur Pendennis; or a gentleman and a tailor, like the Great Mell; or a gentleman and a thief, like many of the founders of our noble families.

The Illustrated London News, 8 October 1910

---

*On p. 102 of her 1930 novel *The Edwardians*, Vita Sackville-West (b. 1892) gives exactly the same sequence of occupations as GKC in what she calls the 'chaplet'. But by the time of my 1940s childhood the list went: 'Tinker, tailor, soldier, sailor, rich man, poor man, beggarman, thief'. – BH

12

AMERICA

AMERICA THE BIG

There are a great many things which I really do admire about America; which I admire with much more sincerity than is common in those who merely flatter America. I admire America for being simple, for not being snobbish, for being still democratic in instincts, for having a respect for work and for treating the mere luxurious cynic as a lounge-lizard. But I do not admire America for being big. I do not envy America for being big.

There is no nation more active than the Americans, none more naturally intelligent, none more easy to move for the purpose of starting a campaign, or spreading an idea. But it is obvious that the field of operations is too large even for the largest campaign. The idea cannot be spread, even spread very thin, over quite so vast a surface.

The Illustrated London News, 10 November 1928

MIND OF STATES

Cyrus Pym belonged to a country in which things are possible that seem crazy to the English . . . Pym knew whole States which are vast and yet secret and fanciful; each is as big as a nation yet as private as a lost village, and as unexpected as an apple-pie bed. States where no man may have a cigarette, States where any man may have ten wives, very strict prohibition States, very lax divorce States – all these large local vagaries had prepared Cyrus Pym's mind for small local vagaries in a smaller country.

Manalive, 1915

MOUNT RUSHMORE

When I first heard of the scheme for carving colossal heads of American heroes out of the everlasting hills, the scheme (I think) of the American sculptor, Mr Borglum, I felt again the thrill first given to me in childhood in reading Nathaniel Hawthorne's fantasy of 'The Great Stone Face'. . . The whole conception really requires the vast American background of prairies and mountain-chains. Anyone will feel, I think, that it would be rather too big for England. It would be rather alarming for the Englishman returning by boat to Dover, to see that Shakespeare's Cliff had suddenly turned into Shakespeare.

The Illustrated London News, 31 October 1931

AMERICA THE YOUNG

Nearly five generations have grown old and grey declaring that America is a young nation. It will probably be the last remark made by the last American when, centuries hence, America sinks into the Atlantic like the lost continent of Atlantis . . . The original motive for insisting that America is young was not only not American, but was distinctly disrespectful to America. It arose from the desire of the Englishman to claim the complete and sole parentage of so enormous an infant; and yet at the same time to patronize the infant, for being so very infantile. It assumed that the American was only an immature English . . . I have never believed a word of it myself . . .

GK's Weekly, 6 December 1930

PLEASE STAY PUT

I have hardly criticized anything in America; I have only suggested that certain very American things should remain in America. When Joan of Arc was asked whether God hated the English, that superstitious peasant replied emphatically in the negative, but added that she thought that God did not want them in France.

The Illustrated London News, 21 April 1928

TEA WITHOUT SYMPATHY

GKC is commenting on an American report that 'the dope that is sending all America to defeat and destruction is nicotine, caffeine and theine'.

. . . I cannot believe that anybody was ever destroyed by an American cup of tea. I have known some travellers who were defeated in endeavouring to get an English one. One of them, a lady I know very well, said on first tasting the beverage in its modified American form: 'Well, if that's the sort of tea we sent you, I don't wonder you threw it into Boston Harbor.'

The Illustrated London News, 3 January 1925

SINCLAIR LEWIS

I . . . think there is a considerable movement of American culture just now, from which we might really have something to learn; only that our commercial journalism is bent on learning the worst from American newspapers instead of the best from American books. The Gospel of the Go-getter is beginning to be boomed in England at precisely the moment when it is beginning to be criticized in America; and just when

Babbitt the Bright Salesman is for the first time being made fun of there, he is for the first time being taken seriously here.*

The Illustrated London News, 30 March 1929

*Sinclair Lewis's novel *Babbitt* was published in 1922.

LINCOLN MEMORIAL (LONDON)

I fear the crowds in the street do not know much more about Abraham Lincoln, after a small group has given him a statue, than they did when a somewhat larger group would have been ready to burn him as a guy. And I am sure the newspapers are quite as wrong about Abraham Lincoln when they belaud him as ever they were when they bespattered him. There was a great deal more to be said for his detractors than his admirers imagine. There was also a great deal more to be said for him than his admirers ever say. He was certainly nothing at all like the ideal and almost divine being whom journalistic rhetoric invokes as if he were a god.

The Illustrated London News, 24 April 1926

ABRAHAM LINCOLN

Lincoln was a man who knew what he wanted in this rare sense, that he could distinguish what he wanted from what he got. Almost alone among politicians, he was an opportunist who was not twisted by his own opportunities.

The Illustrated London News, 17 December 1921

FLAWED HERO

A new biography of Lincoln had just been published.

He really was a hero, but he seems exactly the wrong sort of hero for all his own hero-worshippers. We should be rather surprised if a very quiet and pacific colony of Quakers in a Pennsylvanian village had no other interest in life but the glorification of the great Napoleon, the exultant and detailed description of his battles, the lyrical salute of the cannonade of Austerlitz or the cavalry charges of Wagram. We should think it odd if a company of pagan epicureans, crowned with roses and flushed with wine, had no other thought in the world but a devotion to St Simeon Stylites, for his austerity and asceticism in standing on a pillar in the desert . . . And yet the sort of people who incessantly sing the praises of Abraham Lincoln have got hold of a man quite as incongruous to their own conceptions of a hero – if ever they could turn from imagining the hero to considering the man. The sort of people who are called Puritans perpetually glorify a man who seems to have been in his youth a rather crude sort of atheist, and was famous all his life for telling dirty or profane stories . . . Yes, he was a hero all right; but his hero-worshippers would not think so.

The Illustrated London News, 17 November 1928

PROHIBITION

Prohibition is the latest of all experiments in the newest of all nations. And it has become impossible, in a sense beyond what we mean by impracticable or unjustifiable. It has become intellectually intolerable, just as a contradiction in terms is intellectually intolerable. It has now reached a stage in which the chief champions of the law are those who wish to go on violating it . . . The law against boot-legging reposes almost entirely on the support of the boot-leggers.

The Illustrated London News, 24 March 1928

MORE ON PROHIBITION

The one way in which the great American Republic did really make a public and palpable fool of itself, before all the nations of the earth, was not merely in enforcing a Moslem morality on a Christian people. It was primarily and particularly in making that fad or scruple a part of the Constitution . . . A Constitution is simply the statement of how laws are made. It has no business whatever with saying which laws should be made; still less with saying that one particularly silly law must never be unmade. The Prohibition Amendment was as muddle-headed as the Declaration of Independence was clear-headed. It was as muddle-headed as a man who should mix up a plan of a sausage-machine with a recipe for a sausage.

Even in our most illogical moments [we British] should not venerate a jurist who said, 'I define the British Constitution as consisting of Kings, Lords and Commons, and as something that shall stop the motor-buses making such a noise in Ealing Broadway.'

The Illustrated London News, 28 July 1928

BLACKLEG PETROL?

Henry Ford, to GKC's disgust, had spoken in favour of Prohibition.

. . . It is a rather pleasing fancy to let the mind play with the conception of the Prohibition of Petrol. It would be quite easy to use most of the arguments commonly used in the case of drink; to collect very one-sided statistics about injury to health or division of families or danger to life and limb. To begin with, if there were no petrol traffic, there is always a possibility that Americans might learn to walk. I do not say they would. It is only too probable that some other labour-saving device or invention would come to their rescue before they were driven to so desperate a course. It is only too likely that they might be trailed along the street suspended by hooks from aeroplanes, or hurled all the way down Broadway from a gigantic steel catapult . . . The great social reform of the Prohibition of Petrol would certainly relieve the congestion very much . . . It is infinitely more likely . . . that wars will be waged for the possession of oil-fields than it ever was that they would be waged for the possession of hop-fields.

The Illustrated London News, 22 May 1926

DICKENS'S CLEVEREST WORDS

I am inclined to think . . . that Dickens was never in all his life so strictly clever as he is in the American part of *Martin Chuzzlewit* . . . A slave-owner in the Southern States tells Dickens that slave-owners do not ill-treat their slaves, that it is not to the interest of slave-owners to ill-treat their slaves. Dickens flashes back that it is not to the interest of a man to get drunk, but he does get drunk.

Introduction to Dickens's *Martin Chuzzlewit*, London 1907

HIAWATHA'S OTHER HALF

You cannot alter the sense in which water is common and oil-fields are rare. You cannot give to these recent realistic things that inflexible fictitious use that belongs to the elementary things. Americans as well as American Indians could understand that the beautiful wife of Hiawatha had the beautiful name of Laughing Water, but even Americans would hardly call a beautiful maiden by the name of Giggling Petrol.★

GK's Weekly, 14 February 1931

★If they did rename her, wouldn't they call her Giggling Gas? (or Laughing Gas?) – BH

AMERICAN THRILLERS

The American [police novel] begins with what seems to the conventional Englishman the most savage cynicism and brutality; with policemen furiously browbeating and even brazenly lying; with ruthless descriptions of the Third Degree like descriptions of the Spanish Inquisition; even with officers of the law quite openly planning crimes against those they cannot hold as criminals, and shouting, 'I'll frame you for this!' or 'I'll railroad you to the chair.'

I allow for the exaggeration of fiction; but the point is that the American reader does not apparently react against this falsehood. He accepts it as part of the machinery of a modern story, as he accepts the chain of trolley-buses across New York, not as he would accept the sudden introduction of a flaming dragon with three heads walking down Fifth Avenue.

The Illustrated London News, 11 February 1928

THE PROBLEM OF WEALTH

America will probably be the problem of 1926 as much as Prussia was the problem of 1914. The problem will not be so much of a peril, but it will have its perilous aspect. The weight of wealth in the one case has something of the same effect as the weight of war material and war preparations in the other. It disturbs the balance of the world even when it is not being actually used against it.

The Illustrated London News, 2 January 1926

TOMATO, TOMAYTO

If I dislike England being Americanized, I can fairly claim that I have always protested in the past against America being

Anglicized. I think a nation is never so good as when it is national and never so bad as when it is international.

The Illustrated London News, 2 January 1926

IN DEFENCE OF AMERICAN ISOLATIONISM

[During the First World War] it seemed to be assumed by many Englishmen that the American President, quite apart from his international ideals about saving Europe, had some sort of national obligations about saving England.

The Illustrated London News, 2 January 1926

PRE-COLUMBIAN

Nobody knows, perhaps, how many people have discovered America. In a very interesting little book of essays from Dublin, called *Old Wine and New*, by Conall Cearnach, I have just read the suggestion, which seems not without support, that an Irish missionary discovered it in the Dark Ages.

The Illustrated London News, 22 July 1922

THE MYTH OF THE *MAYFLOWER*

The *Mayflower* is a myth. It is an intensely interesting example of a real modern myth. I do not mean of course that the *Mayflower* never sailed, any more than I admit that King Arthur never lived . . . I do not mean that the incident had no historic interest, or that the men who figured in it had no heroic qualities . . . I mean that there exists in millions of modern minds a traditional image or vision called the *Mayflower*, which has little relation to the real facts. Multitudes of people in England and America . . . think of the *Mayflower* as an origin or archetype like the Ark or at least the Argo. Perhaps it would be an exaggeration to say that they think the *Mayflower* discovered America. Above all, they talk as if the establishment of New England had been the first and formative example of the expansion of England. They believe that English expansion was a Puritan experiment; and that an expansion of Puritan ideas was also the expansion of what have been claimed as English ideas, especially ideas of liberty. The Puritans of New England were champions of religious freedom, seeking to found a newer and freer state beyond the sea, and thus becoming the origin and model of modern democracy. All this betrays a lack of exactitude. It is certainly nearer to exact truth to say that Merlin built the castle at Camelot by magic, or that Roland broke the mountains in pieces with his unbroken sword.

Fancies versus Fads, London 1923

THANKS, BUT NO THANKS

The Americans have established a Thanksgiving Day and celebrate the fact that the Pilgrim Fathers reached America. The English might very well establish another Thanksgiving Day, to celebrate the happy fact that the Pilgrim Fathers left England . . . An ordinary modern liberal, sailing with them, would have found no liberty, and would have intensely disliked almost all that he found of religion. Even Thanksgiving Day itself, though it is now kept in a most kindly and charming fashion by numbers of quite liberal and large-minded Americans, was originally invented, I believe, as a sort of iconoclastic expedient for destroying the celebration of Christmas. The Puritans everywhere had a curious and rabid dislike of Christmas . . .

The Illustrated London News, 28 January 1931

AN AMERICAN PROFESSOR

. . . The famous Professor Smaill . . . was, in his way, very American; he had long fair hair brushed back from his square forehead, long straight features and a curious mixture of preoccupation with a poise of potential swiftness, like a lion pondering absent-mindedly on his next leap.

'The Curse of the Golden Cross' (*The Father Brown Stories*)

THE AMERICAN WORK ETHIC

Americans really respect work, rather as Europeans respect war. There is a halo of heroism about it; and he who shrinks from it is less than a man.

'The Curse of the Golden Cross' (*The Father Brown Stories*)

POSH REPUBLICANS

[A] genuine element of sentiment – historic and almost heroic . . . manages to remain side by side with commercialism in the elder cities on the eastern coast of America. [Moon Crescent] was originally a curve of classical architecture really recalling that eighteenth-century atmosphere in which men like Washington and Jefferson had seemed to be all the more republicans for being aristocrats.

'The Miracle of Moon Crescent' (*The Father Brown Stories*)

DICKENS'S RACISM

Along with [Dickens's] American criticism should really go his very characteristic summary of the question of the Red

Indian . . . Dickens can see nothing in the Red Indian except that he is barbaric, retrograde, bellicose, uncleanly, and superstitious – in short, that he is not a member of the special civilization of Birmingham or Brighton. It is curious to note the contrast between the cheery, nay Cockney, contempt with which Dickens speaks of the American Indian and that chivalrous and pathetic essay in which Washington Irving celebrates the virtues of the vanishing race.

Introduction to Dickens's *American Notes*, London 1908

In mitigation of Dickens's views, GKC points out that 'In the very act of describing Red Indians as devils who, like so much dirt, it would pay us to sweep away, he pauses to deny emphatically that we have any right to sweep them away.'

CIGAR TRAGIC (palindrome)

. . . I may say I can bear witness to this great [American] taboo about tobacco. Of course, numberless Americans smoke numberless cigars. But there does seem to exist an extraordinary idea that ethics are involved in some way . . . I remember once receiving two American interviewers on the same afternoon: there was a box of cigars in front of me, and I offered one to each of them. Their reaction . . . was curious to watch. The first journalist stiffened suddenly and silently, and declined in a very cold voice. He could not have conveyed more plainly that I had attempted to corrupt an honourable man with a foul and infamous indulgence, as if I were the Old Man of the Mountain offering him the hashish that would turn him into an assassin. The second journalist first looked doubtful; then looked sly; then seemed to glance about him nervously, as if wondering whether we were alone; and then said, with a sort of crestfallen and covert smile: 'Well Mr Chesterton, I'm afraid I have the habit.'

The Illustrated London News, 5 February 1927

IN AMERICA WE TRUST

There is a danger that we may now trust too much to an American steam-roller, as we once trusted to a Russian steam-roller. We must get rid of the least lingering notion that we have 'made our contribution' and can now leave everything to the larger population of the West. In that sense it is even more insulting to trust America than it would be to distrust America.

The Illustrated London News, 24 August 1918

'AMERICANIZATION'

The first stanza of a two-stanza poem.

> Britannia needs no Boulevards,
> No spaces wide and gay:
> Her march was through the crooked streets
> Along the narrow way.
> Nor looks she where, New York's seduction,
> The Broadway leadeth to destruction. . .

'Americanization'

GENTLEMAN'S GENTLEMAN

GKC had seen a Jeeves story by P. G. Wodehouse in the Strand Magazine, *illustrated by an English artist; but then he had seen the same story in an American magazine, illustrated by an American artist.*

Because the [*Strand*] artist, like the author, was an Englishman, he knew at once what the real relations of Jeeves and Wooster were. The American illustrator had no notion that such wild monsters could exist in the world; and I don't blame him. He read the story and learned that this guy Wooster wanted to put on rather vivid clothes, and this guy Jeeves had the sense to dissuade him. So he drew Wooster as a grinning booby in loud checks with his hat on one side. He made him a comic idiot; in so doing he made him a cad, and Mr Bertie Wooster was not a cad.

But the fact that this ghastly and gibbering half-wit was undoubtedly a gentleman is even less vital than the fact that the stern and controlling servant is undoubtedly a servant. And the American illustrator has not the most shadowy notion of there being such a thing as a servant. He takes the lowering leather-visaged Jeeves, with his cold disapproval and his crushing obedience, and turns him into a lively little elderly man, with brisk grey hair and a bright smile, looking rather like an old Irish journalist always hovering between a drink and a wink. When he remonstrates about the loud checks, he lifts his hand with a natural oratorical gesture and smiles frankly. He is addressing a Fellow Citizen. Let anyone who knows Jeeves, let alone anyone who knows Britannia and all her Butlers, let anyone who likes or dislikes the Island of the Gentlemen, imagine Mr Jeeves lifting a finger and wagging it at his master!

GK's Weekly, 24 December 1932

WAFFLING

Somebody should protest about the pretence in English magazines that American fiction is a thing merely to be transferred and not translated. I have just seen a story of which the very title was 'The Waffle-Iron', with a note warning the reader of the moral danger of becoming like all the other waffles. Does every English reader know what a waffle-iron is, or even what a waffle is? Has the waffle-iron entered his soul, and is he in serious spiritual danger of being permanently waffled?

The Illustrated London News, 23 September 1922

13
LOVE, SEX, MARRIAGE
(and DIVORCE)

THE COURAGE OF HIS CONVICTIONS

From a letter of GKC to a total stranger asking for advice on marriage,
c. 1909.

Dear Madam,

You ask me first where I get my convictions. Conviction
seems to me to be seeing an idea *solid*; that is, from all sides.
When all sorts of different things seem to point to one thing;
then one believes it. Conviction is *never* narrow. One is never
sure of a thing till one has walked all round it. I have looked
at marriage in my time from nearly every standpoint; including that of the anti-marriage people. Conviction comes when
truths converge . . .

British Library, Add. MSS 73276A

MONOGAMY IN BALHAM

. . . The abstract flies flat in the face of all the facts of experience and human nature. It is not true that a moral custom
cannot hold most men content with a reasonable status, and
careful to preserve it. It is as if we were to say that because
some men are more attractive to women than others, therefore the inhabitants of Balham under Queen Victoria could
not possibly have been arranged on a monogamous model,

143

with one man, one wife. Sooner or later, it might be said, all females would be found clustering round the fascinating few, and nothing but bachelorhood be left for the unattractive many. Sooner or later the suburb must consist of a hundred hermitages and three harems. But this is not the case. It is not the case at present, whatever may happen if the moral tradition of marriage is really lost in Balham. So long as that moral tradition is alive, so long as stealing other people's wives is reprobated or being faithful to a spouse is admired, there are limits to the extent to which the wildest profligate in Balham can disturb the balance of the sexes.

The Outline of Sanity, London 1926

SEX

Upon sex and such matters we are in a human freemasonry; the freemasonry is disciplined, but the freemasonry is free. We are asked to be silent about these things, but we are not asked to be ignorant about them. On the contrary, the fundamental human argument is entirely the other way. It is the thing most common to humanity that is most veiled by humanity.

'On Political Secrecy', *All Things Considered*, London 1908

NO KICKING OVER TRACES

. . . I never could join the young men of my time in feeling what they called the general sentiment of revolt. I should have resisted, let us hope, any rules that were evil . . . [but] I could never mix in the common murmur of that rising generation against monogamy, because no restriction on sex seemed so odd and unexpected as sex itself.

Orthodoxy, London 1909

LOVE

. . . There are no things for which men will make such her-culean efforts as the things of which they know they are unworthy. There never was a man in love who did not declare that, if he strained every nerve to breaking, he was going to have his desire. And there never was a man in love who did not declare also that he ought not to have it.

Heretics, London 1906

TRUE LOVE

You can always tell the real love from the slight by the fact that the latter weakens at the moment of success; the former is quadrupled.

Letter to his fiancée, Frances Blogg, c. 1899, quoted by Maisie Ward, *Gilbert Keith Chesterton*, London 1944

ALTARATION

A man's friends like him but they leave him as he is. A man's wife loves him and is always trying to change him.

Quoted by Maisie Ward, *Gilbert Keith Chesterton*, London 1944

TYING THE KNOT

The modern world . . . refuses to perceive the permanent element of tragic constancy which inheres in all passion, and which is the origin of marriage. Marriage rests upon the fact that you cannot have your cake and eat it; that you cannot lose your heart and have it.

Introduction to Dickens's *David Copperfield*, London 1907

DIVORCE FEASTS

Divorce is a thing which the newspapers now not only advertise, but advocate, almost as if it were a pleasure in itself. It may be, indeed, that all the flowers and festivities will now be transferred from the fashionable wedding to the fashionable divorce. A superb iced and frosted divorce-cake will be provided for the feast, and in military circles will be cut with the co-respondent's sword. A dazzling display of divorce presents will be laid out for the inspection of the company, watched by a detective dressed as an ordinary divorce guest . . . The guests will assemble on the doorstep to see the husband and wife go off in opposite directions; and all will go merry as a divorce-court bell.

Fancies versus Fads, London 1923

CONNUBIAL

Some people when married gain each other. Some only lose themselves.

A speech of 1905, quoted by Maisie Ward, *Gilbert Keith Chesterton*, London 1944

SEX THE TYRANT

. . . Sex cannot be admitted to a mere equality among elementary emotions or experiences like eating and sleeping. The moment sex ceases to be a servant it becomes a tyrant.

St Francis of Assisi, London 1923

SEX NOT A SIN

I read in a 'high-class' review of Miss Rebecca West's book on St Augustine, the astounding statement that the Catholic Church regards sex as having the nature of sin. How marriage can be a sacrament if sex is a sin, or why it is the Catholics who are in favour of birth and their foes who are in favour of birth-control, I will leave the critic to worry out for himself.

St Thomas Aquinas, London 1933

AN INDEX OF LOVE

No one . . . was ever in love without indulging in a positive debauch of humility.

The Defendant, London 1901

DECREE ABSOLUTE

I think . . . we may appeal to the sane and self-respecting people even among those who would permit divorce, that they should tell their weaker brethren not at least to glorify it. It may be a piece of very silly sentimentalism to represent the world as full of happy marriages, but to represent the world as full of happy divorces seems to me much sillier and much more sentimental.

The Illustrated London News, 11 January 1913

14

BEAUTY, DRESS
AND FASHION

UNACCUSTOMED AS WE ARE . . .

If I were asked why I think our whole industrial society is
cursed with sterility and stamped with the mark of the slave,
I could give a good many answers, but one will serve for the
moment: because it cannot create a custom. It can only create
a fashion.

The Illustrated London News, 26 June 1926

BEAUTY

People speak of the pathos and failure of plain women; but it
is a more terrible thing that a beautiful woman may succeed
in everything but womanhood.

Manalive, 1915

SOME SWAN; SOME NECK

The line in the modern version of 'Annie Laurie', 'Her neck
is like the swan', always suggested to me a very startling and
somewhat alarming alteration in the human form . . .

'About Bad Comparisons', *As I Was Saying*, London 1936

FASHION, 1915

The girl in white . . . wore a hat of the proportions of a parachute, which might have wafted her away into the coloured clouds of evening.

Manalive, 1915

MUMMY FIXATION

Lady Miriam was a very long and languid and elegant lady, handsome in a recent fashion largely modelled on Egyptian mummies.

'The Actor and the Alibi' (*The Father Brown Stories*)

FORMALITY

'Always wear uniform, even if it's a shabby uniform!' [cried the obliging person]. 'Ritualists may always be untidy. Go to a dance with soot on your shirt-front; but go with a shirt-front. Huntsman wears old coat, but old pink coat. Wear a topper, even if it's got no top. It's the symbol that counts, old cock.'

Manalive, 1915

DRESS INFORMAL

'But I can't make head or tail of it,' said the doctor. 'You must really begin at the beginning.'

'The beginning of it was a dressing-gown,' said Father Brown simply. 'It was the one really good disguise I've ever known. When you meet a man in a house with a dressing-gown on, you assume quite automatically that he's in his own house . . .'

'The Curse of the Golden Cross' (*The Father Brown Stories*)

ON *HAMLET* IN MODERN DRESS

What we call modern costume is simply the remains of that queer Puritanical convention; and to make Hamlet modern is not in the least to make him more unconventional. It is to make him more conventional.

The Illustrated London News, 12 September 1925

FICKLE FASHION

. . . Fashion, in the feverish sense that it exists today, is . . . a merely destructive thing; indeed, an entirely negative thing. It is as if a man were perpetually carving a statue and smashing it as soon as he carved it . . . It is as if people began to dig up the foundations of a house before they had finished putting the roof on . . .

The Illustrated London News, 26 June 1926

1920s FASHIONS

The figure of the fashionable girl, as compared with the figure of the Venus de Milo, is in every sense of the word a lesser thing. That is, it is, whether beautiful or no, a more limited thing. The short hair of the modern girl is, by its very nature, a limitation. It may be a wise or sensible limitation, as compared with complicated masses of coiled hair, but it is the disappearance of a feature. It is subtraction and not addition. It is making a girl look like a boy; like making an elephant look like a hippopotamus.

The Illustrated London News, 20 October 1928

A SPECTACLE OF HIMSELF

Otherwise the man was exquisitely dressed; and to Brown, in his innocence, the spectacles seemed the queerest disfigurement for a dandy. It was as if a dandy had adorned himself with a wooden leg as an extra touch of elegance.

'The Arrow of Heaven' (*The Father Brown Stories*)

GANDHI'S DRESS

We seem to have discovered that he is a puzzle and therefore decided that he is a joke. The popular press, which was often also the patriotic press, seems unable to get any further than the fact that he wears some sort of white garment; in which respect he sets a good example of decorum and respectability to some of our own Nordic Nudists in Anglo-Saxon model villages or German holiday resorts . . .*

The Illustrated London News, 10 October 1931

*In 1931, Gandhi attended the London Round Table Conference on Indian constitutional reform.

15

EDUCATION

SCHOOL STORIES

Mr Kipling's 'Stalky and Co.' is much more amusing . . . than the late Dean Farrar's 'Eric; or, Little by Little'. But 'Eric' is immeasurably more like real school-life. For real school-life, real boyhood, is full of the things of which Eric is full – priggishness, a crude piety, a silly sin, a weak but continual attempt at the heroic, in a word, melodrama.

Heretics, London 1906

THAT OTHER ETON . . .

'Good God, the Board Schools!'* said Syme. 'Is this undenominational education?'

'No,' said the policeman sadly, 'I never had any of those advantages. The Board Schools came after my time. What education I had was very rough and old-fashioned, I am afraid.'

'Where did you have it?' asked Syme, wondering.

'Oh, at Harrow,' said the policeman.

The Man Who Was Thursday, London 1908

*Board Schools: these were established under the Board of Education set up by the Education Act of 1870 for universal free education. 'Undenominational': there was a continuing dispute as to whether the religious practice of such schools should be Church of England.

EDUCATING THE POOR

There are two modern malcontents who are very often confused together. There is the man who grumbles because the poor are educated and the man who grumbles because they are not.

The Illustrated London News, 18 February 1928

EDUCATIONISTS

The cold suspicious world cannot help remarking that, when the educationist praises a course of education, it is generally that by which he himself can be considered an educated man. It is the cobblers who think the cobbling culture is everything.

The Illustrated London News, 4 August 1928

UNWANTED EDUCATORS

With the high priests of Mumbo-Jumbo I am on friendly terms; with the worshippers of the Green Monkey and the Seven-headed Snake I can chat cheerfully if we meet by chance in society; with the Blood-drinkers of Baphomet I have tactfully agreed to differ; with the Howling Dervishes of the Red Desert I see the road open to reunion; from those who offer their babies to the Most Ancient Crocodile I differ only in opinion; of those who consider it a sign of divine favour that their mother's head is bitten off by a Bengal tiger, I am willing to believe that they are better than their creed; to those who believe the sea to be the green blood of a great giant whose anaemic visage is exhibited in the moon, I am ready to concede that we may be looking at two different aspects of truth . . . But there is one way of informing about such things and such people which seems to me to suggest something utterly sub-human and much less than half-witted . . . something so stupid that we can hardly call it the mind of man . . .

There is something in the grossest idolatry or the craziest mythology that has a quality of groping and adumbration. There is more in life than we understand . . . But the evolutionary educator, having never since his birth been in anything but the dark, naturally believes that he is in the daylight. His very notion of daylight is something which is so blank as to be merely blind. There are no depths to it, either of light or darkness. There are no dimensions in it . . . certainly no dimensions in which the mind can move.

The Illustrated London News, 6 August 1932

THE ABSOLUTE END

There used to be, and possibly is, a mysterious institution for young ladies known as a finishing-school. The chief case against it was that, in certain instances, it meant finishing an education without ever beginning it.

'On Love', *All I Survey*, London 1933

OXBRIDGE

. . . The lads at Oxford and Cambridge are only larking because England, in the depths of its solemn soul, really wishes them to lark. All this is very human and pardonable, and would be even harmless if there were no such things in the world as danger and honour and intellectual responsibility . . . It is not a working way of managing education to be entirely content with the mere fact that you have (to a degree unexampled in the world) given the luckiest boys the jolliest time.

'Oxford from Without', *All Things Considered*, London 1908

16

TRANSPORT

TRAMBIENT

Basil Grant and I were talking one day in what is perhaps the most perfect place for talking on earth – the top of a tolerably deserted tramcar. To talk on the top of a hill is superb, but to talk on the top of a flying hill is a fairy tale.

The Club of Queer Trades, London 1905

NATIONAL SYMBOL

[The hansom cab] is comfortable, and yet it is reckless; and that combination is the very soul of England.*

Tremendous Trifles, London 1909

*Maisie Ward writes (*Gilbert Keith Chesterton*, London 1944): 'In [*The Napoleon of Notting Hill*], the thought of the [hansom] cab moves him to write:

> Poet whose cunning carved this amorous cell
> Where twain may dwell.

E. V. Lucas, his daughter tells us, used to say that if one were invited to drive with Gilbert in a hansom cab, it would have to be two cabs; but this is not strictly true. For in those days I drove with Gilbert and Frances, too, in a hansom – he and I side by side, she on his knee.'

IN DEFENCE OF STRIKES

Take for example the case of a strike on the Tubes. Suppose that at an age of innocence you had met a strange man who had promised to drive you by the force of the lightning through the bowels of the earth . . . Or if we picture it a pneumatic and not an electric railway; suppose he gaily promised to blow you through a pea-shooter to the other side of London Bridge . . . You would at least think that the strange man was a very strange man . . . You might even call him a magician, if he did do it. But the point is this, that you would not call him a Bolshevik merely because he did not do it.

Fancies versus Fads, London 1923

CARS VERSUS TRAINS

The railway is fading before our eyes . . . The railway really was a communal and concentrated mode of travel like that in a Utopia of the Socialists. The free and solitary traveller is returning before our very eyes . . .

The Outline of Sanity, London 1926

GOING TOPLESS

I want to know why next to nobody now has an open motorcar. I want to know why practically all the present makes of motor-cars are . . . on . . . the saloon model. That is, at the very best, they are closed cars that are made to open; rather than open cars that are made to shut . . . It interests me very much, because practically everything that I ever praised, or could praise, or could imagine anybody praising about motoring was bound up with the open car and has vanished with it

. . . There will be fewer types of motor-cars under monopolist mass-production; not more. The best kind of motor-cars will be abandoned, not the worst.

GK's Weekly, 9 January 1932

TRAFFIC JAM

. . . I fear I never like the traffic quite so much as when it stands still. In the middle of a prolonged block in the Uxbridge Road, I have been known to exhibit a gaiety and radiant levity which has made me loathed and detested for miles round. I always feel a faint hope, after a few hours of it, that the vehicles may never move on at all, but may sink slowly into the road and take on the more rooted character of a large and prosperous village.

'About Traffic', *As I Was Saying*, London 1936

17

MURDER AND OTHER CRIMES

MURDER

'The time has gone by', Dr Cyrus Pym said, 'when murder could be regarded as a moral and individual act, important perhaps to the murderer, perhaps to the murdered. Science has profoundly . . .' here he paused, poising his compressed finger and thumb in the air as if he were holding an elusive idea very tight by its tail, then he screwed up his eyes and said 'modified', and let it go – 'has profoundly Modified our view of death. In superstitious ages it was regarded as the termination of life, catastrophic, and even tragic, and was often surrounded by solemnity. Brighter days, however, have dawned, and we now see death as universal and inevitable . . . In the same way we have come to consider murder *socially*.'

Manalive, 1915

VIOLENCE

Place that man in the silver-silent purity of the palest cloister, and there will be some deed of violence done with the crozier or the alb. Rear him in a happy nursery, amid our brave-browed Anglo-Saxon infancy, and he will find some way to strangle with the skipping-rope or to brain with the brick.

Manalive, 1915

INTELLIGENT MURDER

[Horne Fisher:] 'Every intelligent murder involves taking advantage of some one uncommon feature in a common situation. The feature here was the fancy of old Hook for being the first man up every morning, his fixed routine as an angler, and his annoyance at being disturbed . . .'

The Man Who Knew Too Much, London 1922

SELF-EXAMINATION

'I have pretty often had the task of investigating murders, as it happens,' said Father Brown. 'Now I have got to investigate my own murder.'

'If I were you,' said Race, 'I should take a little wine first.'

'The Resurrection of Father Brown' (*The Father Brown Stories*)

FACT AND FANCY

'Of course, dear old Collins said he only wanted the facts. What an absurd blunder! In a case of this kind we emphatically do *not* only want the facts. It is even more essential to have the fancies.'

'The Miracle of Moon Crescent' (*The Father Brown Stories*)

LATE CALL

'Every crime depends on somebody not waking up too soon,' [said] Father Brown; 'and in every sense most of us wake up too late.'

'The Song of the Flying Fish' (*The Father Brown Stories*)

CRIMINOLOGY A SCIENCE?

'My good sir,' said the professor in remonstrance, 'don't you believe that criminology is a science?'

'I'm not sure,' replied Father Brown. 'Do you believe that hagiology is a science?'

'What's that?' asked the specialist sharply.

'No; it's not the study of hags, and has nothing to do with burning witches,' said the priest, smiling. 'It's the study of holy things, saints and so on. You see, the Dark Ages tried to make a science about good people. But our own humane and enlightened age is only interested in a science about bad ones.'

'The Man with Two Beards' (*The Father Brown Stories*)

A WORRYING ELOPEMENT

Father Brown: 'Saving the grace of God, I was very nearly frightened of that woman. But she was frightened of me, too; frightened of something I'd seen or said. Knight was always begging her to bolt with him. Now she's done it; and I'm devilish sorry for him.'

'For him?' enquired Jarvis.

'Well, it can't be very nice to elope with a murderess,' said the other dispassionately.

'The Actor and the Alibi' (*The Father Brown Stories*)

POT, KETTLE

Father Brown: 'No man's really any good till he knows how bad he is, or might be; till he's realized exactly how much right he has to all this snobbery, and sneering, and talking about "criminals", as if they were apes in a forest ten thousand miles away; till he's got rid of all the dirty self-deception of talking about low types and deficient skulls; till he's squeezed out of his soul the last drop of the oil of the Pharisees . . .'

'The Secret of Father Brown' (*The Father Brown Stories*)

FINGERED BY THE LAW

The ultimate effect of the great science of Fingerprints is that whereas a gentleman was expected to put on gloves to dance with a lady, he may now be expected to put on gloves to strangle her.

Avowals and Denials, London 1935

SKULL AND CROSSPATCH

Scientists had just announced that, after extensive investigations, they had found 'There is no such thing as a criminal skull'.

I submit that it was not necessary to collect or count or measure the skulls of criminals in order to discover that there is no such thing as the criminal skull. Anybody with the rudiments of common sense can see for himself that there could not possibly be such a thing as the criminal skull. There could not be, for instance, a man who showed by the shape of his head that he would commit a murder, any more than there could be a man who showed by the shape of his head that he would travel through Clapham Junction.

The Illustrated London News, 10 June 1920

18
DETECTIVE STORIES

A MIRACULOUS DRAUGHT OF RED HERRINGS

. . . The detective novel differs from every other kind of
novel. The ordinary novelist desires to keep his readers to the
point; the detective novelist actually desires to keep his readers
off the point.

Introduction to Dickens's unfinished novel, *The Mystery of Edwin Drood*,
London 1909

MURDER MOST MORAL

[Murder stories] are probably the only books that are still built
on the traditional plan of truth and honour as understood by
all the great civilizations of the past. All the rest are more or
less persuasive apologies for perjury or less attractive presen-
tations of betrayal . . . All the archetypal tales of Scripture, like
Cain and Abel, were of the same kind . . . What bound all
these traditional tales together, true or false, great or small,
was the fact that the moral was the same if the fable was different; and the moral is that murder is a habit to be avoided.

The Illustrated London News, 3 March 1934

NEED FOR A WHODUNIT PRIMER

On detective fiction.

. . . It is all the more curious that the technique of such tales is not discussed, because they are exactly the sort in which technique is nearly the whole of the trick. It is all the more odd that such writers have no critical guidance, because it is one of the few forms of art in which they could to some extent be guided. And it is all the more strange that nobody discusses the rules, because it is one of the rare cases in which some rules could be laid down . . . Nobody writes the simple book which I expect every day to see on the bookstalls, called *How to Write a Detective Story*.

The Illustrated London News, 19 August 1922

SOLVING THE DROOD MYSTERY

Even if we get the right solution we shall not know that it is right.

Introduction to Dickens's unfinished novel, *The Mystery of Edwin Drood*,
London 1909

THE CORPSE IS – THE AUTHOR

. . . Alone, perhaps, among detective-story writers, [Dickens] never lived to destroy his mystery.

Introduction to Dickens's unfinished novel, *The Mystery of Edwin Drood*,
London 1909

A STATUE FOR SHERLOCK

I hope to see the day when there shall be a statue of Sherlock Holmes in Baker Street, as there is a statue of Peter Pan in Kensington Gardens. These are perhaps the only two figures in fiction which have in recent times really become legends . . .

The Illustrated London News, 15 January 1927

INDISPENSABLE, MY DEAR WATSON

In [the] last stories of Sherlock Holmes, though they are not generally so good as the earlier ones, there is at least one rather interesting demonstration. Sherlock Holmes does demonstrate one fact triumphantly: that he cannot do without Watson.

The Illustrated London News, 15 January 1927

UNFAIR TO MYSTERY WRITERS

I see that Mrs Carolyn Wells, the American lady who has produced many of our most charming stories of murder and mystification, has been writing to a magazine to complain of the unsatisfactory sort of review accorded to that sort of book. She says it is only too obvious that the task of reviewing detective stories is given to people who do not like detective stories. She says, and I think not unreasonably, that this is very unreasonable: a book of poems is not given to a man who hates poetry; an ordinary novel is not reviewed by a rigid moralist who regards all novels as immoral.

The Illustrated London News, 19 August 1922

DEAD RICH

It is to be feared that about a hundred detective stories have begun with the discovery that an American millionaire has been murdered, an event which is, for some reason, treated as a sort of calamity.

'The Arrow of Heaven' (*The Father Brown Stories*)

ONE MAN'S POISON . . .

The Detection Club, of which I have the honour to be President, very properly vows each of its members to avoid making a detective story depend on 'mysterious poisons unknown to science'. Unfortunately, most of the poisons known to science would probably be unknown to me . . . I have not even the humble function of being a Consumer . . .

GK's Weekly, 7 March 1935

19

RELIGION

'THE DONKEY'

When fishes flew and forests walked
And figs grew upon thorn,
Some moment when the moon was blood
Then surely I was born.
With monstrous head and sickening cry
And ears like errant wings,
The devil's walking parody
On all four-footed things.
The battered outlaw of the earth,
Of ancient crooked will;
Starve, scourge, deride me: I am dumb,
I keep my secret still.
Fools! For I also had my hour;
One far fierce hour and sweet:
There was a shout about my ears,
And palms before my feet.

'The Donkey'

ORIGINAL SIN

It is not a mere verbal coincidence that original thinkers believe in Original Sin. For really original thinkers like to think about origins.

The Illustrated London News, 1 September 1928

THE FALL

The Fall is a view of life. It is not only the only enlightening, but the only encouraging view of life. It holds, as against the only real alternative philosophies, those of the Buddhist or the Pessimist or the Promethean, that we have misused a good world, and not merely been entrapped into a bad one. It refers evil back to the wrong use of the will, and thus declares that it can eventually be righted by the right use of the will. Every other creed except that one is some form of surrender to fate.

The Thing, New York 1930

SOMETHING TO LIVE UP TO

It is no disgrace to Christianity, it is no disgrace to any great religion, that its counsels of perfection have not made every single person perfect. If after centuries a disparity is still found between its ideal and its followers, it only means that the religion still maintains the ideal, and the followers still need it. But it is not a thing at which a philosopher in his five wits has any reason to be surprised.

The Illustrated London News, 2 March 1929

SUPERSTITIONS OF THE SCEPTICS

The great disadvantage of those who have too much strong sense to believe in supernaturalism is that they keep last the low and little forms of the supernatural, such as omens, curses, spectres and retributions, but find a high and happy supernaturalism quite incredible. Thus the Puritans denied the sacraments, but went on burning witches.

Introduction to Dickens's *Oliver Twist*, London 1907

LETTER OF THE LAW

Christ knew that it would be a more stunning thunderbolt to fulfil the law than to destroy it.

What's Wrong with the World, London 1910

DODGEM DOGMAS

Prejudices are divergent, whereas creeds are always in collision. Believers bump into each other; whereas bigots keep out of each other's way. A creed is a collective thing, and even its sins are sociable. A prejudice is a private thing, and even its tolerance is misanthropic.

What's Wrong with the World, London 1910

MIRACLES

I'm so sorry,' said Father Brown; 'I'm afraid there's some mistake. I don't think I ever said it was a miracle. All I said was that it might happen. What you said was that it couldn't happen, because it would be a miracle if it did. And then it did. And so you said it was a miracle. But I never said a word about miracles or magic, or anything else of the sort from beginning to end.'

'But I thought you believed in miracles,' broke out the secretary.

'Yes,' answered Father Brown, 'I believe in miracles. I believe in man-eating tigers, but I don't see them running about everywhere. If I want any miracles, I know where to get them.'

'The Miracle of Moon Crescent' (*The Father Brown Stories*)

THAT MOMENT OF DOUBT

Christianity is the only religion on earth that has felt that omnipotence made God incomplete. Christianity alone has felt that God, to be wholly God, must have been a rebel as well as a king. Alone of all creeds, Christianity has added courage to the virtues of the Creator. For the only courage worth calling courage must necessarily mean that the soul passes a breaking point – and does not break . . .

In that terrific tale of the Passion there is a distinct emotional suggestion that the author of all things (in some unthinkable way) went not only through agony, but through doubt . . . In a garden Satan tempted man; and in a garden God tempted God. He passed in some superhuman manner through our human horror of pessimism. When the world shook and the sun was wiped out of heaven, it was not at the crucifixion, but at the cry from the cross: the cry which confessed that God was forsaken of God . . . [Atheists] will find only one divinity who ever uttered their isolation; only one religion in which God seemed for an instant to be an atheist.

Orthodoxy, London 1909

SEEING *IS* BELIEVING

We [Christians] shall be left defending, not only the incredible virtues and sanities of human life, but something more incredible still, this huge impossible universe which stares us in the face. We shall fight for visible prodigies as if they were invisible. We shall look on the impossible grass and the skies with a strange courage. We shall be of those who have seen and yet have believed.

Heretics, London 1906

THE BIBLE TRUTH

. . . The quarrels between the Victorian whitewashers and the Post-Victorian mudslingers seem to me deficient in the ordinary decent comprehension of the difficulties of human nature. Both the scandalized and the scandalmongers seem to me to look very silly beside the sensible person in the Bible who confined himself to saying that there are things that no man knows, such as the way of a bird in the air and the way of a man in his youth.

Robert Louis Stevenson, London 1907

UNTESTED

Catholicism was not tried . . . The world did not tire of the church's ideal, but of its reality. Monasteries were impugned not for the chastity of monks, but for the unchastity of monks. Christianity was unpopular not because of the humility, but because of the arrogance of Christians . . . The Reformation began to tear Europe apart before the Catholic Church had had time to pull it together . . . The Christian ideal has not been tried and found wanting. It has been found difficult and left untried.

What's Wrong with the World, London 1910

CROMWELL'S ERROR

Puritanism was an honourable mood; it was a noble fad. In other words, it was a highly creditable mistake.

William Blake, London 1910

TORMENTED

'You do not understand,' replied Father Stephen quite quietly. 'If there are any who stand apart merely because the world is utterly evil, they are not old monks like me; they are much more likely to be young Byronic disappointed lovers like you. No, it is the optimist much more than the pessimist who finally finds the cross waiting for him at the end of his own road. It is the thing that remains when all is said, like the payment after the feast. Christendom is full of feasts, but they bear the names of martyrs who won them in torments. And if such things horrify you, go and ask what torments your English soldiers endure for the land which your English poets praise. Go and see your English children playing with fireworks, and you will find one of their toys is named after the torture of St Catherine. No, it is not that the world is rubbish and that we throw it away. It is exactly when the whole world of stars is a jewel, like the jewels we have lost, that we remember the price. And we look up, as you say, in this dim thicket and see the price, which was the death of God.'

The Man Who Knew Too Much, London 1922

ST PETER

When Christ at a symbolic moment was establishing His great society, He chose for its corner-stone neither the brilliant Paul nor the mystic John, but a shuffler, a snob, a coward – in a word, a man. And upon this rock He has built His Church, and the gates of Hell have not prevailed against it. All the empires and the kingdoms have failed, because of this inherent and continual weakness, that they were founded by strong men and upon strong men. But this one thing, the historic Christian Church, was founded on a weak man, and for that reason it is indestructible. For no chain is stronger than its weakest link.

Heretics, London 1906

JUMPING FOR JOY

Orthodoxy makes us jump by the sudden brink of hell; it is only afterwards that we realize that jumping was an athletic exercise highly beneficial to our health . . . The strongest argument for the divine grace is simply its ungraciousness. The unpopular parts of Christianity turn out when examined to be the very props of the people. The outer ring of Christianity is a rigid guard of ethical abnegations and professional priests; but inside that inhuman guard you will find the old human life dancing like children . . .

Orthodoxy, London 1909

VIRGIN ON THE RIDICULOUS

'Father Brown believes a good number of things, I take it,' said Vandam, whose temper was suffering from the past snub and the present bickering. 'Father Brown believes a hermit crossed a river on a crocodile conjured out of nowhere, and then he told the crocodile to die, and it sure did. Father Brown believes that some blessed saint or other died, and had his dead body turned into three dead bodies, to be served out to three parishes that were all bent on figuring as his home-town. Father Brown believes that a saint hung his cloak on a sunbeam, and another used his for a boat to cross the Atlantic. Father Brown believes the holy donkey had six legs and the house of Loretto flew through the air. He believes in hundreds of stone virgins winking and weeping all day long . . . I reckon he doesn't take much stock of the laws of nature.'

'The Miracle of Moon Crescent' (*The Father Brown Stories*)

THREE IN ONE

If [the] love of a living complexity be our test, it is certainly healthier to have the Trinitarian religion than the Unitarian. For to us Trinitarians (if I may say it with reverence) – to us God Himself is a society.

Orthodoxy, London 1909

GLASTONBURY

In Glastonbury, as in all noble and humane things, the myth is more important than the history . . . The tale that Joseph of Arimathea came to Britain is presumably a mere legend. But it is not by any means so incredible or preposterous a legend as many modern people suppose. The popular notion is that the thing is quite comic and inconceivable; as if one said that Wat Tyler went to Chicago, or that John Bunyan discovered the North Pole . . .

'The Gold of Glastonbury', *Alarms and Discursions*, London 1911

SEEING THROUGH THINGS

. . . I think a broad distinction between the finest pagan and the finest Christian point of view may be found in such an approximate phrase as this, that paganism deals always with a light shining on things, Christianity with a light shining through things.

G. F. Watts, London 1904

PURE NONSENSE

. . . There is every other virtue in Puritanism except purity
. . . It has not many images of positive innocence; of the things
that are at once white and solid, like the white chalk or white
wood which children love.

Robert Louis Stevenson, London 1907

DEARTH OF FAITH

Men have not got tired of Christianity; they have never found
enough Christianity to get tired of.

What's Wrong with the World, London 1910

TOOTHLESS TIGER

GKC is suggesting that Puritanism is dead in Scotland.

[Stevenson], Barrie and Buchan . . . would never have fondled
the tiger-cat of Calvinism until, for them, its teeth were drawn.

Robert Louis Stevenson, London 1907

CALVIN DECLINE

. . . This was the irony and the pathos of the position of Scottish Calvinism: to be rammed down people's throats for three
hundred years as an unanswerable argument and then to be
inherited at the last as an almost indefensible affectation; to be
expounded to boys as a scowl and remembered by men with
a smile . . . All that long agony of lucidity and masterful logic
ended at last suddenly with a laugh; and the laugh was Robert
Louis Stevenson.

Robert Louis Stevenson, London 1907

GODSPELL

It was with more than his usual breeziness that the reverend gentleman on this occasion affirmed the philosophy of his life.

'God wants you to play the game,' he said. 'That's all that God wants; people who will play the game.'

'How do you know?' asked Mr Pond rather snappishly and in unusual irritation. 'How do you know what God wants? You never were God, were you?'

There was a silence; and the atheist was seen to be staring at the red face of the parson in a somewhat unusual fashion.

'Yes,' said the clergyman in a queer quiet voice. 'I was God once; for about fourteen hours. But I gave it up. I found it was too much of a strain.'

The Poet and the Lunatics, London 1929

LOOKING THE PART

Far be it from me to say a word against the Reverend Raymond Percy, the colleague in question. He was brilliant, I suppose, and to some apparently fascinating; but a clergyman who talks like a Socialist, wears his hair like a pianist, and behaves like an intoxicated person, will never rise in his profession, or even obtain the admiration of the good and wise.

Manalive, 1915

PIG HOOEY

A fanatical Islamic prophet is speaking.

'It is to me very strange that the Christians should so laugh and be surprised because we hold ourselves to be defiled by pork; we and also another of the Peoples of the Book. But surely you Christians yourselves consider the pig as a manner of pollution; since it is your most usual expression of your despising, of your very great dislike. You say "swine", my dear lady; you do not say animals far more unpopular, such as the alligator.'

The Flying Inn, London 1914

VOLTAIRE AND AQUINAS

A man like Voltaire happened to begin asking questions at a moment when men had forgotten how to answer them . . . I know of no question that Voltaire asked which St Thomas Aquinas did not ask before him. Only St Thomas not only asked, but answered the questions. When the questions merely hung unanswered in the air, in a restless, worldly and uncontemplative age, there came to be a vague association between wit and that sort of sneering inquiry. In short, there came to be an entirely false association between intelligence and scepticism.

The Illustrated London News, 22 February 1930

ACCIDENT-PRONE

As soon stay the cataracts of the London waterworks as stay the great tendency of Dr Warner to be assassinated by somebody. Place that man in a Quakers' meeting, among the most peaceful of Christians, and he will immediately be beaten to death with sticks of chocolate. Place him among the angels of the New Jerusalem, and he will be stoned to death with precious stones.

Manalive, 1915

RISING UP AND RAISING UP

A Revolution is a mild thing compared with a Resurrection; and nothing less can raise us from the dead.

GK's Weekly, 26 March 1932

DRAWING ON CAPITAL

. . . The modern world, with its modern movements, is living on its Catholic capital. It is using, and using up, the truths that remain to it out of the old treasury of Christendom; including, of course, many truths known to pagan antiquity but crystallized in Christendom. But it is *not* really starting new enthusiasms of its own. The novelty is a matter of names and labels, like modern advertisement; in almost every other way the novelty is merely negative. It is not starting fresh things that it can really carry on far into the future.

The Thing, New York 1930

MURDER IN THE CATHEDRAL

When four knights scattered the blood and brains of St Thomas of Canterbury, it was not only a sign of anger but of a sort of black admiration. They wished for his blood, but they wished even more for his brains.

What's Wrong with the World, London 1910

THE DAMASCUS ROAD OF SCROOGE

A Christmas Carol . . . is not only the story of a conversion, but of a sudden conversion; as sudden as the conversion of a man at a Salvation Army meeting. Popular religion is quite right in insisting on the fact of a crisis in most things. It is true that the man at the Salvation Army meeting would probably be converted from the punch bowl; whereas Scrooge was converted to it.

Introduction to Dickens's *Christmas Books*, London 1907

PIO NONO – A NONO

The case against the Church in Italy in the time of Pio Nono* was not the case which a rationalist would urge against the Church of the time of St Louis, but diametrically the opposite case. Against the medieval Church it might be said that she was too fantastic, too visionary, too dogmatic about the destiny of man, too indifferent to all things but the devotional side of the soul. Against the Church of Pio Nono the main thing to be said was that it was simply and supremely cynical; that it was not founded on the unworldly instinct for distorting life, but on the worldly counsel to leave life as it is; that it was not the inspirer of insane hopes, of reward and miracle, but the enemy, the cool and sceptical enemy, of hope of any kind of description.

Robert Browning, London 1903

*Pius IX (1792–1878), Pope from 1846. The Vatican Council (1869–79) proclaimed papal infallibility.

A DEAD HERESY

Nobody now wants to revive the Divine Right of Kings which the first Anglicans advanced against the Pope.

The Thing, New York 1930

RELIGIOUS KITSCH

We do not say that every pink and blue doll from an Art Repository is a satisfactory symbol of the Mother of God . . . We do not profess to admire the little varnished pictures of waxen angels or wooden children around the Communion Table . . .

The Thing, New York 1930

CORRUPTION AND THE CLOISTER

. . . Even to talk of the corruption of the monasteries is a compliment to the monasteries. For we do not talk of the corruption of the corrupt. Nobody pretends that the medieval institutions began in mere greed and pride. But the modern institution did. Nobody says that St Benedict drew up his rule of labour in order to make his monks lazy; but only that they became lazy. Nobody says that the first Franciscans practised poverty to obtain wealth; but only that later fraternities did obtain wealth. But it is quite certain that the Cecils and the Russells and the rest did from the first want to obtain wealth.

GK's Weekly, 19 May 1928

ALL THINGS BRIGHT AND BEAUTIFUL

All good things are one thing. Sunsets, schools of philosophy, babies, constellations, cathedrals, operas, mountains, horses, poems – all these are merely disguises. One thing is always walking among us in fancy-dress, in the grey cloak of a church or the green cloak of a meadow. He is always behind, His form makes the folds fall so superbly . . . The Greeks and Norsemen and Romans saw the superficial wars of nature and made the sun one god, the sea another, the wind a third. They were not thrilled, as some rude Israelite was, one night in the wastes, alone, by the sudden blazing idea of all being the same God: an idea worthy of a detective story.

Letter to his fiancée, Frances Blogg, 11 July 1899

ON PRAYER

The mountains praise thee, O Lord!

But what if a mountain said, 'I praise thee, But put a pine-tree halfway up on the left; It would be much more effective, believe me.'

It is time that the religion of prayer gave place to the religion of praise.

GKC's Notebook (begun 1894)

OUT, BRIEF CANDLE

Everybody knows that Hugh Latimer, in dying very bravely for his own faith or doubt or transition, made the remark, 'We have this day lit a candle which by God's grace shall never be put out.' It was a curious metaphor for a man who was in fact assisting to put out all the candles on all the altars . . .

GK's Weekly, 2 January 1932

THE BADGE OF THE PROTESTANT

In a chapter headed 'Why I am a Catholic', GKC asserts that most Protestants have forgotten what Protestantism was.

If almost any modern man is asked whether we save our souls solely through our theology, or whether doing good '(to the poor, for instance) will help us on the road to God, he would answer without hesitation that good works are probably more pleasing to God than theology. It would probably come as quite a surprise to him to learn, that, for three hundred years, the faith in faith alone was the badge of a Protestant, the faith in good works the rather shameful badge of a disreputable Papist.

The Thing, New York 1930

THE ACID TEST

The ordinary Englishman . . . if he believes in God at all, or even if he does not, . . . would quite certainly prefer a God who has made all men for joy, and desires to save them all, to a God who deliberately made some for involuntary sin and immortal misery. But that was the quarrel; and it was the Catholic who held the first and the Protestant who held the second.

The Thing, New York 1930

LOSING ONE'S HEAD

With a long and sustained tug we have attempted to pull the mitre off pontifical man; and his head has come off with it.

Orthodoxy, London 1909

THE HELP OF MAN

Men can be frozen by fatalism, or crazed by anarchism, or driven to death by pessimism; for men will not go on indefinitely acting on what they feel to be a fable. And it is in this organic and almost muscular sense that religion is really the help of man — in the sense that without it he is ultimately helpless, almost motionless.

The Thing, New York 1930

NEEDED: LITTLE LATIN AND LESS GREEK

The general notion that science establishes agnosticism is a sort of mystification produced by talking Latin and Greek instead of plain English. Science is the Latin for knowledge. Agnosticism is the Greek for ignorance. It is not self-evident that ignorance is the goal of knowledge.

The Thing, New York 1930

WHERE ARE YOU COMING FROM?

When a man assumes the absurdity of anything that anybody else believes, we wish first to know what he believes . . .

The Thing, New York 1930

REFLECTIONS

Wherever there is water the height of high buildings is doubled, and a British brick house becomes a Babylonian tower . . . There is something pleasing to a mystic in such a land of mirrors. For a mystic is one who holds that two worlds are better than one. In the highest sense, indeed, all thought is reflection.

Manalive, 1915

IDOLS AND EMPERORS

When I asked [Wong-Hi, guardian of a temple in the Forest of Fu] for what he should be forgiven, he answered: 'For being right.'

'Your idols and emperors are so old and wise and satisfying,' he cried, 'it is a shame that they should be wrong. We are so vulgar and violent, we have done you so many iniquities – it is a shame that we should be right after all.'

Manalive, 1915

FROM HERE, NOT ETERNITY

[Innocent Smith:] 'I think God has given us the love of special places, of a hearth and of a native land, for a good reason.'

'I dare say,' [Louis Harn] said, 'What reason?'

'Because otherwise,' he said, pointing his pole out at the sky and the abyss, 'we might worship that.'

'What do you mean?' I demanded.

'Eternity,' he said in his harsh voice, 'the largest of the idols – the mightiest of the rivals of God.'

'You mean pantheism and infinity and all that,' I suggested.

'I mean,' he said with increasing vehemence, '. . . that God bade me love one spot and serve it, and do all things however wild in praise of it, so that this one spot might be a witness against all the infinities and sophistries, that Paradise is some-where and not anywhere, is something and not anything.'

Manalive, 1915

NEVER THE TWAIN SHALL MEET

A Puritan may think it blasphemous that God should become a wafer. A Moslem thinks it blasphemous that God should become a workman in Galilee.

The Thing, New York 1930

THE BASES OF PRAYER

To any atheist, to any rational rationalist, it [is] obvious that prayer does depend on three quite definite dogmas. First, it implies that there is an invisible being, who can hear our prayer without ordinary and material communication; which is a dogma. Second, it implies that the being is benevolent, and not hostile; which is also a dogma. Third, it implies that he is not limited by the logic of causation, but can act in reference to our action; which is a great thundering dogma.

The Illustrated London News, 19 January 1929

THE VOICE OF GOD

There was a cold crash of stillness in the room; and Moon said, '*Pax populi vox Dei*; it is the silence of the people that is the voice of God.'

Manalive, 1915

HOLY TERROR

If we eliminate altogether that awe or fear, or whatever we choose to call it, which there has been in all religions, we do lose along with it much of the joy and poetry of religion. It is possible to be far too much at ease in Zion. It is possible to begin to treat the Holy City as if it were the Hampstead Garden City [*sic*]. And that is a failure even in the fulness of life; for people do not really enjoy Hampstead as much as they should enjoy Heaven.

The Illustrated London News, 9 February 1929

IN OR OUT?

Captain Patrick Dalroy recalls a hole in the heath where he used to have picnics.

'The Hole in Heaven!' he said. 'What a good name! What a good poet I was in those days! The Hole in Heaven! But does it let one in, or let one out?'

The Flying Inn, London 1914

THE DRUIDS

The beginning of a three-stanza poem.

>The Druids waved their golden knives
>And danced around the Oak
>When they had sacrificed a man;
>But though the learned search and scan,
>No single modern person can
>Entirely see the joke.
>But though they cut the throats of men
>They cut not down the tree,
>And from the blood the saplings sprang
>Of oak-woods yet to be . . .

The Flying Inn, London 1914

SACRIFICES

. . . By all the ancient theory of sacrifice, a man should not sacrifice what he does not esteem. Men did not offer dead vultures or decaying rats to the gods, but the best heifer or the spotless lamb. If ascetics have given up love or liberty, it is not because these things are not valuable, but because they are.

The Illustrated London News, 9 February 1929

THE PAGAN GLOW

Paganism may be compared to that diffused light that glows in a landscape when the sun of worship is behind a cloud. So when the true centre of worship is for some reason invisible or vague, there has always remained for healthy humanity a sort of glow of gratitude or wonder or mystical fear, if it were only reflected from ordinary objects or natural forces or fundamental human traditions. It was the glory of the great Pagans, in the great days of Paganism, that natural things had a sort of projected halo of the supernatural. And he who poured wine upon the altar, or scattered dust upon the grave, never doubted that he dealt in some way with something divine . . .

The Illustrated London News, 7 May 1932

SUPERSTITION

'Credulity is a curious thing,' went on Treherne in a low voice. 'It is more negative than positive, and yet it is infinite. Hundreds of men will avoid walking under a ladder; they don't know where the door of the ladder will lead. They don't really think God would throw a thunderbolt at them for such a thing. They don't know what would happen, that is just the point; but yet they step aside as from a precipice.'

The Man Who Knew Too Much, London 1933

COLD AS CHARITY

The modern world was not made by its religion but rather in spite of its religion. Religion has produced evils of its own; but the special evils which we now suffer began with its breakdown. Nor do I mean religion merely in an ideal, but strictly in a historical sense. The cruel competition of classes went with an abandonment of charity – not merely of the primitive theory of charity, but of the medieval practice of charity . . .

The Illustrated London News, 5 July 1919

WEIGHING THE EVIDENCE

Many supernatural stories rest on the evidence of rough unlettered men, like fishermen and peasants; and most criminal trials depend on the detailed testimony of quite uneducated people. It may be remarked that we never throw a doubt on the value of ignorant evidence when it is a question of a judge hanging a man, but only when it is a question of a saint healing him.

The Illustrated London News, 30 August 1919

SEEING THE FUNNY SIDE

It is the test of a good philosophy whether you can defend it grotesquely. It is the test of a good religion whether you can joke about it.

When I was a very young journalist I used to be irritated at a peculiar habit of printers, a habit which most persons of a tendency similar to mine have probably noticed also. It goes along with the fixed belief of printers that to be a Rationalist is the same thing as to be a Nationalist. I mean the printer's tendency to turn the word 'cosmic' into the word 'comic'. It annoyed me at the time. But since then I have come to the conclusion that the printers were right. The democracy is always right. Whatever is cosmic is comic.

'Spiritualism', *All Things Considered*, London 1908

SNAKE-OIL RELIGIONS

'Oh; I've sized up those religions of the future,' said the millionaire, contemptuously. 'I've been through them with a tooth-comb and they're as mangy as yellow dogs. There was that woman called herself Sophia: ought to have called herself Sapphira, I reckon. Just a plum fraud. Strings tied to all the tables and tambourines. Then there were the Invisible Life bunch; said they could vanish when they liked, and they did vanish, too, and a hundred thousand of my dollars vanished with them. I knew Jupiter Jesus out in Denver, saw him for weeks on end; and he was just a common crook . . . No, I'm through with all that; from now on I only believe what I see. I believe they call it being an atheist.'

'The Miracle of Moon Crescent' (*The Father Brown Stories*)

HE GOT GOD

He was one of those laymen who are much more ecclesiastical than ecclesiastics.

'The Resurrection of Father Brown' (*The Father Brown Stories*)

A TEST OF RELIGION

If any one wandering about wants to have a good trick or test for separating the wrong idealism from the right, I will give him one on the spot. It is a mark of false religion that it is always trying to express concrete facts as abstract; it calls sex affinity; it calls wine alcohol; it calls brute starvation the economic problem. The test of true religion is that its energy drives exactly the other way; it is always trying to make men feel truths as facts; always trying to make abstract things as plain and solid as concrete things; always trying to make men, not merely admit the truth, but see, smell, handle, hear and devour the truth. All great spiritual scriptures are full of the invitation not to test, but to taste; not to examine, but to eat.

'The Appetite of Earth', *Alarms and Discursions*, London 1911

ATHEISM – THE LATIN WAY

There had recently swept through that region [the north coast of South America] one of those fevers of atheist and almost anarchist Radicalism which break out periodically in countries of the Latin culture, generally beginning in a secret society and generally ending in a civil war and in very little else.

'The Resurrection of Father Brown' (*The Father Brown Stories*)

THE SMILE OF SATANISM

Father Brown: 'I know something about Satanism, for my sins; I've been forced to know. I know what it is, what it practically always is. It's proud and it's sly. It likes to be superior; it loves to horrify the innocent with things half understood, to make children's flesh creep. That's why it's so fond of mysteries and initiations and secret societies and all the rest of it. Its eyes are turned inwards, and however grand and grave it may look, it's always hiding a small, mad smile.'

'The Miracle of Moon Crescent' (*The Father Brown Stories*)

A CIGAR FOR QUEEN VICTORIA

Father Brown: 'It really is more natural to believe a preternatural story, that deals with things we don't understand, than a natural story that contradicts things we do understand. Tell me that the great Mr Gladstone, in his last hours, was haunted by the ghost of Parnell, and I will be agnostic about it. But tell me that Mr Gladstone, when first presented to Queen Victoria, wore his hat in her drawing-room and slapped her on the back and offered her a cigar, and I am not agnostic at all. That is not impossible; it's only incredible. But I'm much more certain it didn't happen than that Parnell's ghost didn't appear, because it violates the laws of the world I understand.

'The Curse of the Golden Cross' (*The Father Brown Stories*)

IN DENIAL

A villain is speaking of the superstition that the Devil can only be killed with a silver bullet.

'You do believe it,' he said. 'You do believe everything. The deniers believe. The unbelievers believe. Don't you feel in your heart that these contradictions do not really contradict: that there is a cosmos that contains them all? The soul goes round upon a wheel of stars and all things return; . . . even . . . eternal hatred is an eternal love. Good and evil go round in a wheel that is one thing and not many. Do you not realize in your heart, do you not believe behind all your beliefs, that there is but one reality and we are its shadows, and that all things are but aspects of one thing: a centre where men melt into Man and Man into God?'

'No,' said Father Brown.

'The Curse of the Golden Cross' (*The Father Brown Stories*)

LÈSE-DIVINITÉ

. . . Men can endure a man who behaves as if he were the Devil better than a man who behaves as if he were God. And they are theologically right; for the latter man is not only copying the rebel angel, but copying his act of rebellion.

GK's Weekly, 17 July 1926

GOOD HEAVENS!

We are all supposed to be trying to walk into heaven; but we should be uncommonly astonished if we suddenly walked into it.

'The White Horses', *Alarms and Discursions*, London 1911

BEGGING TO DIFFER

There is a phrase of facile liberality uttered again and again at ethical societies and parliaments of religion: 'the religions of the earth differ in rites and forms, but they are the same in what they teach'. It is false: it is the opposite of the fact. The religions of the world do *not* greatly differ in rites and forms; they do greatly differ in what they teach . . . The difficulty of all the creeds of the earth is not as alleged in this cheap maxim: that they agree in meaning, but differ in machinery. It is exactly the opposite. They agree in machinery; almost every great religion on earth works with the same external methods, with priests, scriptures, altars, sworn brotherhoods, special feasts. They agree in the mode of teaching; what they differ about is the thing to be taught.

Orthodoxy, London 1909

THE DEVIL

One of the oldest and newest . . . ideas . . . about the spiritual struggle is this – that the devil is a traitor. It is more dangerous to be his friend than to be his foe.

The Illustrated London News, 19 September 1935

NO ANGELS IN ARCHANGEL

A paragraph in the newspapers reports, I know not with how much truth, that the Minister controlling education in the present Russian régime has ordered the elimination of references to angels, devils, and even fairies . . .

Perhaps Horatio will avoid the mention of angels by saying to the dying Hamlet, 'Good-night, sweet prince; and flights of scientists sing thee to thy rest.' But I gather from the same context that the phrase 'sweet prince' would also be open to objection; as one of the educational principles there laid down is that 'princely heroes' are to be shown in their true colours as despots and oppressors. In that case Horatio will have to say 'sour prince' . . .

The Illustrated London News, 20 April 1921

NO DOUBT IT'S NOT TRUE

Truths turn into dogmas the instant that they are disputed. Thus every man who utters a doubt defines a religion.

Heretics, London 1906

DEUS EX MACHINA?

Lord Inglewood refers to an episode at Brakespeare College, Cambridge, in the recallable past.

The young men of that sad time thought that the god always came from the machine. They did not know that in reality the machine only comes from the god.

Manalive, 1915

THE IMPOSSIBLE v. THE IMPROBABLE

'Well,' said Tarrant, 'it's refreshing to find a priest so sceptical of the supernatural as all that.'

'Not at all,' replied the priest calmly; 'it's not the supernatural part I doubt. It's the natural part. I'm exactly in the position of the man who said, "I can believe the impossible, but not the improbable."'

'The Curse of the Golden Cross' (*The Father Brown Stories*)

ACCENTUATE THE NEGATIVE

St Francis is a very strong example of this quality in the man of genius, that in him even what is negative is positive, because it is part of a character. An excellent example of what I mean may be found in his attitude towards learning and scholarship. He ignored and in some degree discouraged books and book-learning; and from his own point of view and that of his own work in the world he was absolutely right. The whole point of his message was to be so simple that the village idiot could understand it.

St Francis of Assisi, London 1923

SOMETHING LIKE LOVE

. . . To this great mystic his religion was not a thing like a theory but a thing like a love-affair.

St Francis of Assisi, London 1923

ST FRANCIS

. . . He suffered fools gladly.

St Francis of Assisi, London 1923

A MAN: A PLAN: A CANONIZATION

You can make a sketch of St Francis: you could only make a plan of St Thomas, like the plan of a labyrinthine city.

St Thomas Aquinas, London 1933

CURE OF SOULS

The saint is a medicine because he is an antidote. Indeed, that is why the saint is often a martyr: he is mistaken for a poison because he is an antidote.

St Thomas Aquinas, London 1933

OPPOSITES ATTRACT

. . . Each generation is converted by the saint who contradicts it most . . . In a world that was too stolid, Christianity returned in the form of a vagabond [St Francis]; in a world that has grown a great deal too wild, Christianity has returned in the form of a teacher of logic [St Thomas Aquinas].

St Thomas Aquinas, London 1933

FIGHT PEOPLE ON THEIR OWN TERMS

After the great example of St Thomas, the principle stands, or ought always to have stood established; that we must either not argue with a man at all, or we must argue on his grounds and not ours.

St Thomas Aquinas, London 1933

INTOLERABLE

Generally, the difficulty is not to tolerate other people's religion. The trouble is to tolerate our own religion. Or rather (to speak more strictly) to get our own religion to tolerate us. Comparatively few modern religions are intolerant. But a great many modern religious people are intolerable.

The Illustrated London News, 31 May 1913

THE CURSE AGAINST GOD

Profanity is now more than an affectation – it is a convention. The curse against God is Exercise I in the primer of poetry.

The Wild Knight and Other Poems, London 1900

DID PROTEST TOO MUCH

Long after we have let drop the fancy that Protestantism was rational it will be its glory that it was fanatical.

George Bernard Shaw, London 1910

STAGE FRIGHTS

The discussion about religion on the stage has already sown wind and reaped whirlwind . . . If we were suddenly asked, 'Shall an Ethiopian slave be in a dressing-room?' most of us would have the intelligence to ask first, 'Whose slave in whose dressing-room?' But when people say, 'Should Religion be in a Theatre?' nobody seems to have the intelligence to ask, 'Whose religion in whose theatre?' If the religion of the Quakers (which consists of quietitude and listening for an inner voice) were presented at the Moulin Rouge, I should think it unfair to the Quakers. If, on the other hand, the religion of the Thugs (which consists of strangling people) were practically presented at the Comedy Theatre, I should think it unfair to the Comedy Theatre. There cannot, in the flat face of history, be any Christian objection to Bible stories being presented as plays. According to many learned and devout scholars, they actually were plays.

The Illustrated London News, 27 September 1913

THE SITE OF EDEN

It is a strange thing that many truly spiritual men, such as General Gordon, have actually spent some hours in speculating upon the precise location of the Garden of Eden. Most probably we are in Eden still. It is only our eyes that have changed.

The Defendant, London 1901

THE GREATEST RELIGIOUS POEM

. . . In the greatest religious poem existent, the Book of Job, the argument which convinces the infidel is not (as has been represented by the merely rational religionism of the eighteenth century) a picture of the ordered beneficence of the Creation; but, on the contrary, a picture of the huge and undecipherable unreason of it.

The Defendant, London 1901

NO PLAY

A Puritan meant originally a man whose mind had no holidays.

George Bernard Shaw, London 1910

LESS HOLY THAN THOU

The holy man always conceals his holiness; that is the one invariable rule.

St Thomas Aquinas, London 1933

THE MOST HELLISH HELL

The one hell which imagination must conceive as most hellish is to be eternally acting a play without even the narrowest and dirtiest greenroom in which to be human.

The Defendant, London 1901

TOUCHÉ!

A very honest atheist with whom I once debated made use of the expression, 'Men have only been kept in slavery by the fear of hell.' As I pointed out to him, if he had said that men had only been freed from slavery by the fear of hell, he would at least have been referring to an unquestionable historical fact.

St Francis of Assisi, London 1923

NOT EVEN SIMILAR

It is a real case against conventional hagiography that it sometimes tends to make all saints seem to be the same. Whereas in fact no men are more different than saints; not even murderers,

St Thomas Aquinas, London 1933

20

MISCELLANEOUS

PARADOXES

All my life, or at least the later part of it, I have been trying to discover the meaning of the word 'paradox'. It seems to have two meanings – a statement that seems to contain a contradiction or to be intrinsically improbable, and a statement that happens to be different from the catchwords common at a moment. Now, as a fact, these catchwords themselves are often intrinsically contradictory or improbable. So that, by the simple operation of stating the dull and obvious truth, one may gain quite a picturesque reputation for dashing and dazzling paradox.

The Illustrated London News, 1 August 1925

PROPHECIES

People are always prophesying what will happen next; and they are always falling into the fatuous and obvious folly of making it merely the same as what happened last. As the French King was certainly more powerful in the seventeenth century than in the sixteenth century, everybody would have prophesied that at the end of the eighteenth century he would be more powerful still. At the end of the eighteenth century he had ceased to exist.

The Illustrated London News, 17 March 1928

TERROR TOYS

GKC had been told that fewer bows and arrows were being made for little boys, because those toys were considered dangerous.

. . . Of all the things a child sees and touches, the most dangerous toy is about the least dangerous thing. There is hardly a single domestic utensil that is not much more dangerous than a little bow and arrows. He can burn himself in the fire, he can boil himself in the bath, he can cut his throat with the carving-knife, he can scald himself with the kettle, he can choke himself with anything small enough, he can break his neck off anything high enough . . . He plays all day in a house fitted up with engines of torture like the Spanish Inquisition. And while he thus dances in the shadow of death, he is to be saved from all the perils of possessing a piece of string, tied to a bent bough or twig.

Fancies versus Fads, London 1923

OVER-PROTECTION

. . . You do not keep a little boy from throwing stones by preventing him from ever seeing stones. You do not do it by locking up all the stones in the Geological Museum, and only issuing tickets of admission to adults. You do not do it by trying to pick up all the pebbles on the beach . . . You trust to your private relation with the boy, and not to your public relation with the stone.

Fancies versus Fads, London 1923

TORTURE

I believe that in heathen Rome, the model of a merely civic and secular loyalty, it was the common practice to torture the slaves of any household subjected to legal enquiry. If you had remon-strated, because no crime had been proved against the slaves, the State would have answered in the modern manner: 'We are not punishing the crime; we are protecting the community.'

Fancies versus Fads, London 1923

POLICE STATEMENT

'Ours is the only trade', said [the policeman] Bagshaw, 'in which the professional is always supposed to be wrong. After all, people don't write stories in which hairdressers can't cut hair and have to be helped by a customer; or in which a cabman can't drive a cab until his fare explains to him the philosophy of cab-driving.'

'The Mirror of the Magistrate' (*The Father Brown Stories*)

IN FOR THE KILL

GKC has been in Spain.

. . . I did not go to see any bull-fights, for a reason which I explained to my Spanish friends on the spot. I said I should be very much annoyed if one of my Spanish friends came to England, and instantly put on pink that he might rush to the meet and be in at the death of a poor little fox, and then turn round and say: 'How hideous! How repulsive! What brutes in human form are the English, whose whole lives are passed in this degrading sport!' We can indulge in all sorts of controversy and casuistry about bull-fighting or fox-hunting, and there is a great deal to be said against both. But, whatever is the right way of treating a bull or a fox, there is a very wrong way of treating a man or a nation of men. And that is to make your first dash to see something that you know you will dislike, in order to tell him that you dislike it.

The Illustrated London News, 19 June 1926

IF ONLY HE HAD KNOWN

A man might possibly learn to appreciate machines from a book; whereas I gravely doubt whether the most patient pupil would ever learn to appreciate books from a machine.

The Illustrated London News, 4 August 1928

BEWARE OF *IDÉES FIXES*

When a man clings to one fact, against the tide and torrent of the whole truth, when he sets his feet firmly on one passion or one power, against commonsense and even his own instincts about the nature of things, when he answers everything by saying, 'I have the bond; I have one promise; I have the formula', it is indeed true that his own talisman will almost certainly fail him.

The Illustrated London News, 19 September 1925

This statement anticipates the thinking of the Austrian-born British philosopher Karl Popper. One cannot help wondering how far it might apply to GKC's Roman Catholic beliefs.

MAN IS NOT JUST AN ANIMAL

When we look at [a man] for the very first time, in the full and frank use of our commonsense, we never *do* look at him as an animal . . . If somebody said, 'There is another animal in the garden', and you found it was the Vicar, you would be surprised . . .

The Illustrated London News, 31 October 1925

WHAT IS VULGARITY?

Most of us must have wondered if we could find a real definition of Vulgarity. For it is generally difficult to destroy, or even to defy, a thing that we cannot define . . . It is by the showing off that we see how little there is to show . . . In other words, a thing is only vulgar when its best is base. If [vulgar men] had not been so clever, we might never have known that they were fools. If they had not been so gentlemanly, we should not have seen that they were cads . . . Men are judged by their dreams.

The Illustrated London News, 8 June 1929

THE *FIN DE SIÈCLE*

My first impulse to write, and almost my first impulse to think, was a revolt of disgust with the Decadents and the aesthetic pessimism of the 'nineties. It is now almost impossible to bring home to anybody, even to myself, how final that *fin de siècle* seemed to be; not the end of the century but the end of the world. To a boy his first hatred is almost as immortal as his first love. He does not realize that the objects of either can alter; and I did not know that the twilight of the gods was only a mood. I thought that all the wit and wisdom in the world was banded together to slander and depress the world, and in becoming an optimist I had the feelings of an outlaw.

Fancies versus Fads, London 1923

OPPOSITION

. . . It is absurd to ask a Government to *provide* an opposition. You cannot go to the Sultan and say reproachfully, 'You have made no arrangements for your brother dethroning you and seizing the Caliphate.' You cannot go to a medieval king and say, 'Kindly lend me two thousand spears and one thousand bowmen, as I wish to raise a rebellion against you.' Still less can you reproach a Government which professes to set up everything, because it has not set up anything to pull down all it has set up.

The Outline of Sanity, London 1926

PROPERTY

Property is a point of honour. The true contrary of the word 'property' is the word 'prostitution'. And it is not true that a human being will always sell what is sacred to that sense of self-ownership, whether it be the body or the boundary.

The Outline of Sanity, London 1926

SELF-HELP

. . . Writing one's own love-letters or blowing one's own nose: these things we want a man to do for himself, even if he does them badly.

Orthodoxy, London 1909

THROUGH A GLASS LIGHTLY

. . . To be breakable is not the same as to be perishable. Strike a glass, and it will not endure an instant; simply do not strike it, and it will endure a thousand years.

Orthodoxy, London 1909

'DO IT AGAIN'

Because children have abounding vitality, because they are in spirit fierce and free, therefore they want things repeated and unchanged. They always say, 'Do it again'; and the grown-up person does it again until he is nearly dead. For grown-up people are not strong enough to exult in monotony.

Orthodoxy, London 1909

COMPARISONS NOT ODIOUS

There is nothing that really indicates a subtle and in the true sense a superior mind so much as this power of comparing a lower thing with a higher and yet that higher with a higher still . . .

The Everlasting Man, London 1925

BEST END

. . . A story is exciting because it has in it so strong an element of will, of what theology calls free-will. You cannot finish a sum how you like. But you can finish a story how you like. When somebody discovered the Differential Calculus, there was only one Differential Calculus he could discover. But when Shakespeare killed Romeo he might have married him to Juliet's old nurse if he had felt inclined. And Christendom has excelled in the narrative romance exactly because it has insisted on the theological free-will.

Orthodoxy, London 1909

UNCLUBBABLE

When London was smaller, and the parts of London more self-contained and parochial, the club was what it still is in villages . . . Then the club was valued as a place where a man could be sociable. Now the club is valued as a place where a man can be unsociable. The more the enlargement and elaboration of our civilization goes on, the more the club ceases to be a place where a man can have a noisy argument, and becomes more and more a place where a man can have what is somewhat fantastically called a quiet chop . . . The club tends to produce the most degraded of all combinations – the luxurious anchorite, the man who combines the self-indulgence of Lucullus with the insane loneliness of St Simeon Stylites.

Heretics, London 1906

OFF PRESCRIPTION

. . . In order that life should be a story or romance to us, it is necessary that a great part of it, at any rate, should be settled for us without our permission . . . A man has control over many things in his life; he has control over enough things to be the hero of a novel. But if he had control over everything, there would be so much hero that there would be no novel.

Heretics, London 1906

MARS ISN'T MARVELLOUS

. . . I read in huge headlines, in a daily paper, that one day we shall all visit Mars. I feel just as if I were told that one day we shall all visit Margate. I have heard so much about Mars and Martians, in innumerable romances, shockers, short stories, publications by cranks, revelations by spooks, that I feel as if I knew the place backwards, and had found it a wilderness of advertisements. I am sure you can buy little pink mugs inscribed with 'A Present from Mars'. . . The very fact that the writers always fix on this one particular planet, and never on any other planet, marks the maddening monotony of the whole type of mind.

The Illustrated London News, 23 July 1932

HOPE SPROUTS ETERNAL

I was walking the other day in a kitchen garden, which I find has somehow got attached to my premises, and I was wondering why I liked it. After a prolonged spiritual self-analysis I came to the conclusion that I like a kitchen garden because it contains things to eat. I do not mean that a kitchen garden is ugly; a kitchen garden is often very beautiful. The mixture of green and purple on some monstrous cabbage is much subtler and grander than the more freakish and theatrical splashing of yellow and violet on a pansy.

'The Appetite of Earth', *Alarms and Discursions*, London 1911

THIS TAKES THE BISCUIT

GKC is annoyed when, in a large London restaurant, a waiter brings him cheese 'cut up into contemptibly small pieces', and with biscuits instead of bread.

I asked him if, when he said his prayers, he was so supercilious as to pray for his daily biscuits.

'Cheese', *Alarms and Discursions*, London 1911

BOYS

Those who interpret schoolboys as merely wooden and barbarous, unmoved by anything but a savage seriousness about tuck or cricket, make the mistake of forgetting how much of the schoolboy life is public and ceremonial, having reference to an ideal; or, if you like, to an affectation. Boys, like dogs, have a sort of romantic ritual which is not always their real selves. And this romantic ritual is generally the ritual of not being romantic; the pretence of being much more masculine and materialistic than they are. Boys in themselves are very sentimental. The most sentimental thing in the world is to hide your feelings; it is making too much of them. Stoicism is the direct product of sentimentalism; and schoolboys are sentimental individually, but stoical collectively.

'Simmons and the Social Tie', *Alarms and Discursions*, London 1911

JOY

GKC has been admiring the furrows of a ploughed field, 'like arrows'.

Those cataracts of cloven earth; they were done by the grace of God. I had always rejoiced in them; but I had never found any reason for my joy. There are some very clever people who cannot enjoy the joy unless they understand it. There are other and even cleverer people who say that they lose the joy the moment they do understand it.

'The Furrows', *Alarms and Discursions*, London 1911

LESS DELIGHTFUL IN THE FLESH

I have never managed to lose my old conviction that travel narrows the mind . . . There is something touching and even tragic about the thought of the thoughtless tourist, who might have stayed at home loving Laplanders, embracing Chinamen and clasping Patagonians to his heart in Hampstead or Surbiton but for his blind and suicidal impulse to see what they looked like.

What I Saw in America, London 1922

RAISING CAIN (AND ABEL)

From GKC's letter to the total stranger who asked for advice on marriage, c. 1909.

Two things terribly necessary to mankind are the commonwealth and the family. Somehow Cain and Abel must be brought up and somehow (if possible) Cain must be restrained from killing Abel.

British Library, Add. MSS 73276A

ETERNAL CITIES

Empires pass away almost as if to accentuate the fact that cities do not pass away. At least five empires have successively claimed suzerainty over little Jerusalem upon the hill; and they are all now mere names – Egypt and Babylon and Persia and Macedonia and Rome . . . But Jerusalem is not unimportant . . . Paris is older than France, and York is older than England; and Cologne is immeasurably older than Germany, let alone the German Empire. These centres of civilization have something in them more magnetic and immortal than mere nationality . . . The world ebbs back again in its cities . . .

The Illustrated London News, 11 January 1930

INVESTING IN FUTURES

Anybody may draw any number of blank cheques on the bank of the future. Anybody may run up any number of bills for posterity to discharge when we are all dead, and cannot be charged with anything . . .

The Illustrated London News, 13 April 1929

TO THINE OWN ELF BE TRUE

. . . The ordinary orthodox person is he to whom the heresies can appear as fantasies. After all, it is we ordinary human and humdrum people who can enjoy eccentricity as a sort of elfland; while the eccentrics are too serious even to know that they are elves.

Fancies versus Fads, London 1923

A SPOT-ON PREDICTION

We are already drifting horribly near to a New War, which will probably start on the Polish Border. The young men have had nineteen years in which to learn how to avoid it. I wonder whether they do know much more about how to avoid it than the despised and drivelling Old Men of 1914. How many of the Young Men, for instance, have made the smallest attempt to understand Poland? How many would have anything to say to Hitler, to dissuade him from setting all Christendom aflame by a raid on Poland? Or have the Young Men been thinking of *nothing* since 1914 except the senile depravity of the Old Men of that date?

'On Old Men Who Make Wars', *All I Survey*, London 1933

INCH AND ELL

Among the numberless fictitious things that I have fortunately never written, there was a little story about a logical maiden lady engaging apartments in which she was not allowed to keep a cat or dog, who, nevertheless, stipulated for permission to keep a bird, and who eventually walked round to her new lodgings accompanied by an ostrich.

Fancies versus Fads, London 1923

SERAPH ON A STRING

Suppose whenever a man lit a cigarette, a towering genie arose from the rings of smoke and followed him everywhere as a huge slave. Suppose whenever a man whistled a tune he 'drew an angel down' and had to walk about for ever with a seraph on a string. These catastrophic images are but faint parallels to the earthquake consequences that Nature has attached to sex . . .

What's Wrong with the World, London 1910

PUBLIC RELATIONS

If I find that a limited company is an unlimited swindle, I do not go about cleansing the name of Guatemalan Gutta Perchas or Pekin Consolidated Pork. These names were never sacred to me even when I trusted them; now I distrust them they are nothing at all.

The Illustrated London News, 14 January 1928

PIRATES

If I have to choose between plutocracy and piracy, I prefer the pirates; for that sort of crime necessitated some sorts of virtue. The pirate who grew rich on the high seas at least could not be a coward; the pirate who grows rich on the high prices may be that, as well as everything else that is unworthy.

The Illustrated London News, 7 January 1928

SMUGGLERS

The old smugglers were actually called Free Traders; and there are still a good many Free Traders who would be morally much improved by becoming smugglers.

The Illustrated London News, 7 January 1928

STATING THE OBVIOUS

On psychological tests that had been made into 'Why do people fear?'

Our ancestors might have assumed, in their simplicity, that a man fears a man-eating tiger because it has a tendency to eat a man. They might have been content to say that a man fears a pistol because being shot at is often an approximation to being shot.

The Illustrated London News, 27 February 1926

EVOLUTIONARY

Evolution meant different things to different people; it was sometimes understood as progress towards a perfection in which the lion would lie down with the lamb; it was sometimes understood as a mere ruthless struggle for life in which the lamb could only lie down inside the lion.

The Illustrated London News, 8 August 1931

PLAYING THE FOOL

When the Englishman rediscovered the noble function of making a fool of himself, he did not dress up as an English Merry-Andrew or Jack-in-the-Green. He went to a fancy-dress ball dressed up as a French clown called Pierrot.

The Illustrated London News, 19 February 1927

ATTACK FROM WITHIN

Invasion may be a sword; but powerful penetration is a poison; and some of us would as soon die by Prussian bayonets as by prussic acid. To attack the culture is to attack the country, but it is to attack it from within.

The Illustrated London News, 9 April 1927

SLO-MO

[There is] one sort of moving picture that happens to move me. And it is that in which the whole modern scientific tendency is reversed, and things are made slower than they are instead of quicker than they are. That really does touch the nerve of wonder at the very nature of things. To see a horse jump a five-barred gate ought to be a wonderful thing. But to see a horse climb laboriously into the air, and then crawl slowly through the air, does make vivid to us the vital marvel of his being in the air at all.

The Illustrated London News, 19 March 1927

BROADCASTING PARLIAMENT

The first impulse of an enlightened person on hearing the proposal to broadcast the debates of Parliament is merely that it is one of the typical triumphs of modern science. It is telling us that everybody can listen to what nobody wants to hear.

The Illustrated London News, 4 April 1925

TO THE POINT

Nothing is so bright and cheering as a hostile statement that is really to the point; an opponent who does really see the point, even if he points at it in derision . . . Such a critic sees the same facts that we do, but he sees them in contrasted colours. Most critics do not see the facts at all.

The Illustrated London News, 9 February 1929

FALSEHOODS HARD TO EXPOSE

There are statements of truth of which we can say that they are worse than untrue, for they are unreal. It would be untrue to say that I am writing this article on a scroll of priceless vellum with a golden pen encrusted with diamonds. But it would be unreal to say I am composing it on a flute or a flageolet in the solitude of a woodland glade. The first would be something in the same category as the truth – something that might be true but is not. The second would be something altogether out of touch with the truth – something having no relation to the realities of the senses or the way in which the words reach the reader. But, though in this way unreality is something wilder than untruth, it is sometimes possible for a thing to be in this spectral sense unreal without being in the literal sense untrue. This sort of falsehood is by far the most difficult to expose . . .

The Illustrated London News, 17 November 1923

G. K. CHESTERTON, MP?

I remember being in Paris during a political election, and attaching myself ardently to the cause of a gentleman of the name of Baube*. If I remember right, he proclaimed his politics, as with the blast of a trumpet, in the following words: 'Deputé Radical Républicain Anti-Blocard Socialiste Anti-Collectiviste'. That is the sort of man I am. That is the sort of expression which it would be necessary for the happy crowd to cry in one voice, if it elected me to Parliament. I am a Radical Nationalist Anti-Imperialist Anti-Collectivist Distributivist Christian Social Democrat. I am all that; and there are about three more of me.

The Illustrated London News, 16 July 1921

*See footnote on page 272.

THE *TITANIC*

The Titanic *had sunk on 15 April 1912.*

Quite apart from the question of whether anyone was to blame, the big outstanding fact remains – that there was no sort of sane proportion between the extent of the provision for luxury and levity and the extent of the provision for need and desperation. The scheme did far too much for prosperity and far too little for distress – just like the modern State.

The Illustrated London News, 27 April 1912

OMINOUS CALM

'If we are calm,' [said] the policeman, 'it is the calm of organized resistance.'

'Eh?' said Syme, staring.

'The soldier must be calm in the thick of the battle,'

pursued the policeman. 'The composure of an army is the anger of a nation.'

The Man Who Was Thursday, London 1908

MIRROR, MIRROR ON THE WALL . . .

Up to a point, I am willing to be excited when they discuss what is the most popular song or the most beautiful woman; though I never saw the picture of a prizewinner in any Beauty Competition without thinking that I knew several better-looking women living in my own street.

'About Blondes', *As I Was Saying*, London 1936

BRAIN POWER

What we call the intellectual world is divided into two types of people – those who worship the intellect and those who use it. There are exceptions; but, broadly speaking, they are never the same people.

The Thing, New York 1930

CATS

There are things in this world of which I can say seriously that I love them but I do not like them . . . Cats are the first thing that occur to me as examples of the principle. Cats are so beautiful that a creature from another star might fall in love with them, and so incalculable that he might kill them . . .

To me, unfortunately perhaps (for I speak merely of individual taste), a cat is a wild animal. A cat is Nature personified. Like Nature, it is so mysterious that one cannot quite repose even in its beauty.

Daily News, 12 August 1911

THE FORCE THAT DRIVES . . .

There are realms in which ideas and force rule respectively and separately; but ideas cannot expel force from its own realm except by entering that realm. The limitations of force are that it cannot prevent an idea from being an idea but it can prevent it from being a fact.

The Illustrated London News, 6 July 1918

FREE LOVE

. . . The free lover is simply a person attempting the impossible idea of having a series of honeymoons and no marriage. He is building a long arcade consisting entirely of gates; with no house at the end of them. As he is always trying to repeat the sexual part of the programme, and not go on to the non-sexual part of it, it would seem mere lunacy to say that he is freed from the obsession of sex.

GK's Weekly, 29 January 1927

VENAL OR VENIAL?

If there is one thing worse than the modern weakening of major morals it is the modern strengthening of minor morals. Thus it is considered more withering to accuse a man of bad taste than of bad ethics. Cleanliness is not next to godliness nowadays, for cleanliness is made an essential and godliness is regarded as an offence . . . I have met Ibsenite pessimists who thought it wrong to take beer but right to take prussic acid.

Tremendous Trifles, London 1909

THE OPTIMIST

It is true that men have shrunk from the sting of a great satirist as if from the sting of an adder. But it is equally true that men flee from the embrace of a great optimist as from the embrace of a bear. Nothing brings down more curses than a real benediction. For the goodness of good things, like the badness of bad things, is a prodigy past speech; it is to be pictured rather than spoken.

Manalive, 1915

FLEDGLING NOTIONS

. . . Ideas do most harm while they are still young and before they have been christened.

GK's Weekly, 10 July 1926

SECOND THOUGHTS

Second thoughts are best. Animals have no second thoughts: man alone is able to see his own thought double, as a drunkard sees a lamp-post; man alone is able to see his own thought upside-down as one sees a house in a puddle.

Manalive, 1915

STRENGTH

If an elephant were as strong as a grasshopper, he could (I suppose) spring clean out of the Zoological Gardens and alight trumpeting upon Primrose Hill.

Manalive, 1915

OBSTACLES

Existence with such a man was an obstacle race made of pleasant obstacles.

Manalive, 1915

BRAINED

He undoubtedly had brains; and perhaps it was not his fault if they were the kind of brains that most men desire to analyse with a poker.

Manalive, 1915

PACIFISTS AT WAR

Pacifists do not want Peace; what they want is War with people who are not Pacifists . . . It is a cruel injustice to Pacifists to accuse them of Pacifism. Their inspiration is not mere material peace, but something much nobler; it is hatred, which is a thing of the immortal spirit. It is a perfectly sincere and solid hatred of the sort of things that go with a military culture . . . They hate all those things whose excesses are in the love of glory, which Balzac called 'the sun of the dead'; and whenever they smell that sort of gunpowder, they are quite honestly and almost physically sick.

GK's Weekly, 11 April 1931

GARDEN CITY

The French have no front gardens; but the street is every man's front garden. There are trees in the street, and sometimes fountains. The street is the Frenchman's tavern, for he drinks in the street. It is his dining-room, for he dines in the street. It is his British Museum, for the statues and monuments in French streets are not, as with us, of the worst, but of the best, art of the country . . .

Tremendous Trifles, London 1909

VICTORY FROM THE JAWS OF DEFEAT

It is remarkable that in so many great wars it has been the defeated who have won. The people who were left worst at the end of the war were generally the people who were left best at the end of the whole business. For instance, the Crusades ended in the defeat of the Christians. But they did not end in the decline of the Christians; they ended in the decline of the Saracens. That huge prophetic wave of Moslem power which had hung in the very heavens above the towns of Christendom, that wave was broken, and never came on again. The Crusaders had saved Paris in the act of losing Jerusalem. The same applies to that epic of Republican war in the eighteenth century to which we Liberals owe our political creed. The French Revolution ended in defeat: the kings came back across a carpet of dead at Waterloo. The Revolution had lost its last battle; but it had gained its first object. It had cut a chasm. The world has never been the same since. No one after that has ever been able to treat the poor merely as a pavement . . . The Boers lost the South African War and gained South Africa.

Tremendous Trifles, London 1909

GLORY IN WAR

. . . It is bosh in the abstract, it is bosh in the absolute sense, to say there is no heroism in war because there is so much horror in war. [At the end of dreary novels we find] the inevitable catchword 'There is nothing glorious about war.' . . . It is as if a man were to say 'There is nothing noble about martyrdom. You imagine, I suppose, that St Catherine was perfectly cosy and happy when being broken on the wheel; but I assure you it was most uncomfortable. You are under the impression, no doubt, that St Lawrence thoroughly enjoyed being broiled on a gridiron, but, if you try it, you will find it is really quite tiresome.'

The Illustrated London News, 20 February 1932

THE UNFORGIVABLE SIN

In a recent discussion on Suicide, an interesting comparison was made between what is loosely called the Latin culture and what is still more loosely, and less consistently, called the Nordic or Teutonic or Germanic, according to the foreign policy at the moment. A learned writer pointed out, very truly, that for some reason or other Nordic men are more liable to kill themselves than are the men of the Mediterranean. The men of the Mediterranean are more likely to relieve their feelings by killing somebody else. And in this, I grieve to say, they have a certain half-involuntary support in my sympathies. I admit that murder must be classed among acts distinctly improper and, indeed, morally wrong. But suicide seems to me the supreme blasphemy against God and man and beast and vegetables; the attack not upon a life, but upon life itself . . .

The Illustrated London News, 16 April 1932

DON'T TAKE IT AS READ

When I had looked at the lights of Broadway by night, I made to my American friends an innocent remark that seemed for some reason to amuse them. I had looked, not without joy, at that long kaleidoscope of coloured lights arranged in large letters and sprawling trade-marks, advertizing everything, from pork to pianos, through the agency of the the two most vivid and most mystical of the gifts of God: colour and fire. I said to them, in my simplicity: 'What a glorious garden of wonders this would be, to anyone who was lucky enough to be unable to read.'

What I Saw in America, London 1922

A PROPHETIC RAPTURE

The whole difference between construction and creation is this: that a thing constructed can only be loved after it is constructed; but a thing created is loved before it exists . . . In created art the essence of a book exists before the book or before even the details or main features of the book; the author enjoys it and lives with it with a kind of prophetic rapture.

Introduction to Dickens's *The Pickwick Papers*, London 1907

SEEING THE JOKE

A good joke is the one ultimate and sacred thing which cannot be criticized. Our relations with a good joke are direct and even divine relations. We speak of 'seeing' a joke just as we speak of 'seeing' a ghost or a vision. If we have seen it, it is futile to argue with it.

Introduction to Dickens's *The Pickwick Papers*, London 1907

MUSIC AND FOOD DON'T MIX

. . . It is not greedy to enjoy a good dinner, any more than it is greedy to enjoy a good concert. But I do think there is something greedy about expecting to enjoy the dinner and the concert at the same time . . . The fashion of having very loud music during meals in restaurants and hotels seems to me a perfect example of [the] chaotic attempt to have everything at once and do everything at once.

The Illustrated London News, 18 August 1923

YES WE CAN

There is one metaphor of which the moderns are very fond; they are always saying, 'You can't put the clock back.' The simple and obvious answer is 'You can.' A clock, being a piece of human construction, can be restored by the human finger to any figure or hour. In the same way society, being a piece of human construction, can be reconstructed upon any plan . . .

What's Wrong with the World, London 1910

KNOW YOUR ENEMY

The sincere controversialist is above all things a good listener. The really burning enthusiast never interrupts, he listens to the enemy's arguments as eagerly as a spy would listen to the enemy's arrangements.

What's Wrong with the World, London 1910

INDOOR PICNIC

I often [eat my meals on the floor in my own house]; it gives a curious, childish, poetic, picnic feeling. There would be considerable trouble if I tried to do it in an ABC tea-shop . . .* For a plain, hard-working man the home is . . . the one wild pleasure in the world of rules . . .

What's Wrong with the World, London 1910

*ABC: Aerated Bread Company: it had a chain of tea-shops.

THE NOBLEST WORDS OF ALL

I remember a roomful of Socialists literally laughed when I told them that there were no two nobler words in all poetry than Public House. They thought it was a joke.

What's Wrong with the World, London 1910

SOUL CONSIDERATION

Nothing is important except the fate of the soul; and literature is only redeemed from an utter triviality, surpassing that of naughts and crosses,* by the fact that it describes not the world around us or the things on the retina of the eye or the enormous irrelevancy of encyclopaedias, but some condition to which the human spirit can come.

Introduction to Dickens's *The Old Curiosity Shop*, London 1907

*For American readers: this is the game you call 'Tic-tac-toe'.

MY TROUBLE AND STRIFE

. . . The wise old fairy tales never were so silly as to say that the prince and the princess lived peacefully ever afterwards. The fairy tales said that the prince and princess lived happily ever afterwards: and so they did. They lived happily, although it is very likely that from time to time they threw the furniture at each other. Most marriages, I think, are happy marriages; but there is no such thing as a contented marriage. The whole pleasure of marriage is that it is a perpetual crisis.

Introduction to Dickens's *David Copperfield*, London 1907

DON'T TUT-TUT AT SMUT

I believe firmly in the value of all vulgar notions, especially of vulgar jokes. When once you have got hold of a vulgar joke, you may be certain that you have got hold of a subtle and spiritual idea. The men who made the joke saw something deep which they could not express except by something silly and emphatic. They saw something delicate which they could only express by something indelicate.

The Illustrated London News, 7 March 1908

A CROCLY CROC

We speak of a manly man, but not of a whaley whale. If you wanted to dissuade a man from drinking his tenth whisky, you would slap him on the back and say, 'Be a man.' No one who wished to dissuade a crocodile from eating his tenth explorer would slap it on the back and say, 'Be a crocodile.'

The Religious Doubts of Democracy, London 1903

THE CRITIC'S RÔLE

Criticism does not exist to say about authors the things that they knew themselves. It exists to say the things about them which they did not know themselves. If a critic says that the *Iliad* has a pagan rather than a Christian pity, or that it is full of pictures made by one epithet, of course he does not mean that Homer could have said that. If Homer could have said that, the critic would leave Homer to say it. The function of criticism, if it has a legitimate function at all, can only be one function – that of dealing with the subconscious part of the author's mind which only the critic can express, and not with the conscious part of the author's mind, which the author himself can express. Either criticism is no good at all (a very defensible position) or else criticism means saying about an author the very things that would have made him jump out of his boots.

Introduction to *The Old Curiosity Shop*, reprinted in *Criticisms and Appreciations of the Works of Charles Dickens*, London 1933

A CLEAN BREAST

I believe in getting into hot water. I think it keeps you clean.

Speech made in 1901, quoted by Maisie Ward,
Gilbert Keith Chesterton, London 1944

TIDYING UP

GKC's fiancée, Frances Blogg, tried in the 1890s to persuade him to dress more neatly.

I admit . . . that you are not engaged to the Kosmos: dear me! what a time the Kosmos would have! All its Comets would have their hair brushed every morning. The Whirlwind would be adjured not to walk about when it was talking. The Oceans would be warmed with hot-water pipes. Not even the lowest forms of life would escape the crusade of tidiness: you would walk round and round the jellyfish, looking for a place to put in shirt-links.

Letter to Frances Blogg, postmarked 29 September 1899

THE CARPENTER

The Meditation of Marcus Aurelius.
Yes: he was soliloquizing, not making something.
Do not the words of Jesus ring
Like nails knocked into a board
In his father's workshop?

GKC's Notebook (begun 1894)

IGNORANCE WAS BLISS

As a young man, I knew all about politics and nothing about politicians.

Quoted by Maisie Ward, *Gilbert Keith Chesterton*, London 1944

BUCKING GENDER

Many modern adventures have befallen the more or less tautological maxim that boys will be boys . . . We have even heard modern murmurs of the opposite defect, in complaints that boys won't be boys.

The Illustrated London News, 29 August 1931

MODERATION CAN SEEM TREASON

When a great nation is defending itself against a powerful and oppressive enemy in a great war, it is not in the least unnatural that mere moderation has all the effects of treason.

The Illustrated London News, 20 February 1926

DRAWBACKS OF A HAPPY CHILDHOOD

I regret that I have no gloomy and savage father to offer to the public gaze as the true cause of all my tragic heritage; no pale-faced and partially poisoned mother whose suicidal instincts have cursed me with the temptations of the artistic temperament. I regret that there was nothing in the range of our family much more racy than a remote and mildly impecunious uncle; and that I cannot do my duty as a true modern, by cursing everybody who made me whatever I am.

Autobiography, London 1936

ANSWERING BACK

A cosmos one day being rebuked by a pessimist replied, 'How can you who revile me consent to speak by my machinery? Permit me to reduce you to nothingness and then we will discuss the matter.' Moral. You should not look a gift universe in the mouth.

Letter to Edmund Clerihew Bentley, *c.* 1894

CHESTERTON VILLAGE, CAMBS.

I have never been to Cambridge except as an admiring visitor; I have never been to Chesterton at all, either from a sense of unworthiness or from a faint superstitious feeling that I might be fulfilling a prophecy in the countryside. Anyone with a sense of the savour of the old English country rhymes and tales will share my vague alarm that the steeple might crack or the market cross fall down, for a smaller thing than the coincidence of a man named Chesterton going to Chesterton.

Introduction to M. E. Jones's *Life in Old Cambridge*, Cambridge 1920

NATIONAL SHAVINGS

The best league or mutiny I know of just now is that of the British barbers. 'The Amalgamated Society of British Hairdressers' has sent forth from its central office in the Swan and Sugar Loaf, Fetter Lane, a document addressed to all the citizens of these islands, warning them 'in all seriousness to pause and think before again patronizing a foreign barber'. I never mind pausing and thinking in any time or place; it is my favourite outdoor sport. As a rule, however, I prefer to pause and think while patronizing a foreign barber, or rather – to describe the social relations more correctly – while he is patronizing me.

The Illustrated London News, 10 April 1909

THE ROAD TO HELL

The satirist is the man who carries men's enthusiasm further than they carry it themselves. He outstrips the most extravagant fanatic. He is years ahead of the most audacious prophet. He sees where men's detached intellect will eventually lead them, and he tells them the name of the place – which is generally hell.

Introduction to Dickens's *Martin Chuzzlewit*, London 1907

'RACE-MEMORY (By a dazed Darwinian)'

The last stanza of a six-stanza poem.

> . . . The past was bestial ignorance:
> But I feel a little funky,
> To think I'm further off from heaven
> Than when I was a monkey.

'Race-Memory'

PANIC LEADS TO NONSENSE

Whenever we are in a great period of panic, we are always in a great period of nonsense.

The Illustrated London News, 20 February 1926

FOREIGNERS

The foreigner is not so much a man who ultimately gives a different answer, as a man who begins by asking a different question.

The Illustrated London News, 11 February 1928

AGAINST LUXURY

The sort of sentiment I want the politicians to study, not without tears, took some such form as this: 'Beware of Luxury, the eternal enemy of Liberty.'

The Illustrated London News, 3 March 1928

BELIEF

I can always believe a thing more easily if I have picked up five or six hints of it in general reading, than if I have read the most logical monograph by the most learned man . . . The monograph may be a monomania.

The Illustrated London News, 7 April 1928

ENGLAND v. FRANCE

The Englishman said he had a realm on which the sun never set; and the Frenchman retorted that it was an island on which the sun never rose.

The Illustrated London News, 21 July 1928

BEGINNINGS

I have a senile interest in the beginnings of things – in quaint questionings about why things exist, and whence they came, and what they were really supposed to be. I admit that a bungalow may be made out of a railway carriage, but I am not content that all mankind should live in railway carriages without ever having heard of railways.

The Illustrated London News, 3 March 1928

PROGRESS A MIRAGE

We do not see in the past a perpetual line of increasing liberation or enlargement of artistic experiment. What we see in the past is the much more human business of men first doing something badly; then doing it well; then doing it too well – or, at least, too easily and too often.

The Illustrated London News, 6 October 1928

OVER THE TOP

It is generally agreed that, whatever it was that the French Revolution did, it overdid it.

GK's Weekly, 4 April 1931

SANITY AND SATIRE

. . . Sanity [is] the condition of satire. It is because Gulliver is a man of moderate stature that he can stray into the land of the giants and the land of the pygmies. It is Swift and not the professors of Laputa who sees the real romance of getting sunbeams out of cucumbers.

Fancies versus Fads, London 1923

WHEELS

A wheel is the sublime paradox; one part of it is always going forward and the other part is always going back. Now this, as it happens, is highly similar to the proper condition of any human soul or any political state. Every sane soul or state looks at once backwards and forwards; and even goes backwards to come on.

'The Wheel', *Alarms and Discursions*, London 1911

SET IN STONE

It is an eternal truth that the fathers stone the prophets and the sons build their sepulchres; often out of the same stones.

'On the Staleness of Revolt', *All I Survey*, London 1933

LE MOT JUSTE

. . . Who made the names of the common wild flowers? They were ordinary people, so far as any one knows, who gave to one flower the name of the Star of Bethlehem and to another and much commoner flower the tremendous title of the Eye of Day . . . It will be said that this poetry is peculiar to the country populace [but] ordinary London slang is full of witty things said by nobody in particular . . .

Who first invented these violent felicities of language? Who first spoke of a man 'being off his head'? The obvious comment on a lunatic is that his head is off him; yet the other phrase is far more fantastically exact.

'The Red Town', *Alarms and Discursions*, London 1911

GKC goes on to applaud the expression 'painting the town red'. Also, 'mafficking' − 'The slaves of that saturnalia were not only painting the town red; they thought that they were painting the map red − that they were painting the world red.'

. . . NOR THE YEARS CONDEMN

. . . As far as I know, mere depression never does come from mere age . . . The spirits of the old do not as a rule seem to become more and more ponderous until they sink into the earth. Rather the spirits of the old seem to grow lighter and lighter until they float away like thistledown.

Introduction to Dickens's *Little Dorrit*, London 1908

I DO NOT LOVE YOU . . .

Critics today describe how much they dislike things, rather than why they dislike them.

GKC draws a parallel between this trait and Thomas Brown's adaptation of one of Martial's epigrams –

> *I do not love you, Dr Fell,*
> *But why I cannot tell;*
> *But this I know full well,*
> *I do not love you, Dr Fell.*

The Illustrated London News, 26 September 1931

THE FALLACY OF SOCIALISM

A Socialist means a man who thinks a walking-stick like an umbrella because they both go into the umbrella-stand. Yet they are as different as a battle-axe and a bootjack. The essential idea of an umbrella is breadth and protection. The essential idea of a stick is slenderness and, partly, attack. The stick is the sword, the umbrella is the shield . . . If I might pursue the figure of speech, I might briefly say that the whole Collectivist error consists in saying that because two men can share an umbrella, therefore two men can share a walking-stick . . . There is nothing but nonsense in the notion of swinging a communal stick; it is as if one spoke of twirling a communal moustache.

What's Wrong with the World, London 1910

GKC continues by pointing out the difference between a communal laundry and a communal kitchen. 'Kitchens and wash-houses are both large rooms full of heat and damp and steam. But there is only one right way of washing a shirt; but many ways of cooking . . .' A man might want his sausages well frizzled, but not his shirts.

PREJUDICE AND POSTJUDICE

It never does a man any very great harm to hate a thing that he knows nothing about. It is the hating of a thing when we do know something about it which corrodes the character . . . Prejudice, in fact, is not so much the great intellectual sin as a thing which we may call, to coin a word, 'postjudice', not the bias before the fair trial, but the bias that remains afterwards.

Robert Browning, London 1903

WHEN THE TILTING STOPS

People who are ready to shed tears of sympathy, when the windmills overthrow Don Quixote, are very angry indeed when Don Quixote really overthrows the windmills.

'Essay on Poland', British Library Add. MSS 73261

FINDING ONE'S DIRECTION

Youth is universal, but not individual. The genius who begins life with a very genuine and sincere doubt whether he is meant to be an exquisite and idolized violinist, or the most powerful and eloquent Prime Minister of modern times, does at last end by making the discovery that there is, after all, one thing, possibly a certain style of illustrating Nursery Rhymes, which he can really do better than anyone else.

Robert Browning, London 1903

GIFT OF THE GAB

There are two kinds of men who monopolize conversation. The first kind are those who like the sound of their own voice;

the second are those who do not know what the sound of their own voice is like.

Robert Browning, London 1903

HE SUDDENLY SAW THE DARK

It is nothing that a man dwells on the darkness of dark things; all healthy men do that. It is when he dwells on the darkness of bright things that we have reason to fear some disease of the emotions.

Introduction to Dickens's *Little Dorrit*, London 1908

PAIN BARRIER

In everything worth having, even in every pleasure, there is a point of pain or tedium that must be survived, so that the pleasure may revive and endure. The joy of battle comes after the first fear of death; the joy of reading Virgil comes after the bore of learning him; the glow of the sea-bather comes after the shock of the sea bath; the success of the marriage comes after the failure of the honeymoon.

What's Wrong with the World, London 1910

JIGGERY POKERY

Idealism only means that we should consider a poker in reference to poking before we discuss its suitability for wife-beating . . .

What's Wrong with the World, London 1910

FUTURE IMPERFECT

Futurity does not exist, because it is still future.

What's Wrong with the World, London 1910

WRONG END OF THE STICK

My dear Charles,

I originally called this book 'What is Wrong' and it would have satisfied your sardonic temper to note the number of social misunderstandings that arose from the use of the title. Many a mild lady visitor opened her eyes wide when I remarked casually, 'I have been doing "What Is Wrong" all this morning.'. . .

Dedication to CFG Masterman of *What's Wrong with the World*, London 1910

MOMENT OF TRUTH

There is only one moment, at most, of triumph for the original thinker; while his thought is an originality and before it becomes merely an origin.

Robert Louis Stevenson, London 1907

THE POETIC IMPULSE

It is always the prosaic person who demands poetic subjects. They are the only subjects about which he can possibly be poetic.

Robert Louis Stevenson, London 1907

WHAT'S THE HURRY?

. . . There is one element which must always tend to oligarchy – or rather to despotism; I mean the element of hurry. If the house has caught fire a man must ring up the fire engine; a committee cannot ring them up. If a camp is surprised by night, somebody must give the order to fire; there is no time to vote it . . . Discipline means that in certain frightfully rapid circumstances, one can trust anybody so long as he is not everybody.

What's Wrong with the World, London 1910

HIS FEMININE SIDE

Individually, men may present a more or less rational appearance, eating, sleeping, and scheming. But humanity as a whole is changeful, mystical, fickle, delightful. Men are men, but Man is a woman.

The Napoleon of Notting Hill, London 1904

LEISURE THE ENEMY OF LIBERTY

It is very essential to realize that leisure is not in any way identical with liberty. If we do not realize it, we shall almost certainly all lose our liberty, for any reasonably intelligent tyrant may have the sense to give us a great deal of leisure.

The Illustrated London News, 14 July 1932

NO RULES FOR SELLERS

[In the late nineteenth century] the spotlight of social importance passed from the buyer to the seller. Almost all codes of morals or manners, from the Ten Commandments to the Declaration of Independence, had been conceived from the point of view of the consumer. There was not then a new set of rules or commandments intended to inspire the trader . . . The proof of the pudding was no longer in the eating; indeed, the Age of Suggestion does not condescend to proof.

The Illustrated London News, 13 February 1932

THE AGE OF PSYCHOLOGY

Everybody understands by this time, I imagine, that our age is specially the Age of Psychology, and therefore not the Age of Philosophy. Or, if we prefer to put the point otherwise, it is the Age of Suggestion and therefore not the Age of Reason. The world does not ask whether propositions are proved, but only whether people are persuaded.

The Illustrated London News, 13 February 1932

FAIRIES TO THE RESCUE

Fairy tales do not give the child his first idea of bogey. What fairy tales give the child is his first clear idea of the possible defeat of bogey. The baby has known the dragon intimately ever since he had an imagination. What the fairy tale provides for him is a St George to kill the dragon.

Tremendous Trifles, London 1909

BIRTH CONTROL

I despise Birth-Control first because it is a weak and wobbly and cowardly word . . . The proceeding that quack doctors recommend does not control any birth. It only makes sure that there shall never be any birth to control. It cannot, for example, determine sex . . .

GK's Weekly, 12 November 1932

IRELAND

Ireland is unique in many things; above all, I am glad to say, it is quite unique in the history of England.

GK's Weekly, 21 May 1932

ODDITY

'Have you noticed anything odd about Smith?'

'Well, really,' cried Inglewood, left behind in a collapse of humour, 'have I noticed anything else about him?'

Manalive, 1915

RIDDLES

'Why does everybody repeat riddles,' went on Moon abruptly, 'even if they've forgotten the answers? Riddles are easy to remember because they are hard to guess.'

Manalive, 1915

POSITIVE INACTION

'You are impatient with your elders, Miss Duke; but when you are as old yourself you will know what Napoleon knew

– that half one's letters answer themselves if you can only refrain from the fleshly appetite of answering them.'

Manalive, 1915

KEEPING MUM

Though she never spoke, she always looked as if she might speak any minute.

Manalive, 1915

SLUMMING IT

Moon did not drink . . . but was simply a gentleman who liked low company.

Manalive, 1915

DEATH

[Dr Cyrus Pym:] 'My opponent will at least admit that death is a fact of experience.'

'Not of mine,' said [Michael] Moon mournfully, shaking his head. 'I've never experienced such a thing in all my life.'

Manalive, 1915

SANTA CLAUS

In every well-appointed gentleman's house, I reflected, there was the front door for the gentlemen, and the side door for the tradesmen; but there was also the top door for the gods. The chimney is, so to speak, the underground passage between earth and heaven. By this starry tunnel Santa Claus manages – like the skylark – to be true to the kindred points of heaven and home.

Manalive, 1915

CERTAINLY NOT

The question is whether a man can be certain of anything at all. I think it is impossible he can be certain, for if intellectually to entertain certainty, what is this certainty which it is impossible to entertain? . . . I open my intellect as I open my mouth, in order to shut it again on something solid.

Tremendous Trifles, London 1909

HATCHET MAN

When a man will not bury the hatchet, people always assume it must merely be an axe to grind.

GK's Weekly, 14 August 1926

A PIPE DREAM

A little while ago the newspapers made a fuss about a phrase of Mr Bernard Shaw; something to the effect that smokers should be prosecuted as public nuisances. The obvious difficulty is that the public is itself the nuisance . . . I implore GBS to put this in his pipe and smoke it.

GK's Weekly, 18 December 1926

PERMISSIVENESS

. . . The next great heresy is going to be an attack on morality, and especially on sexual morality.

GK's Weekly, 19 June 1926

IT HAD TO BE ME

An idealist means one who idealizes himself. With more exactitude, he may be defined as one who, when asked to describe the ideal, always describes himself.

GK's Weekly, 17 December 1927

IN THE POST

GKC is opposing George Bernard Shaw's concept of nationalization.

Nobody says anything else about postage stamps. I cannot imagine that anyone wants to have his own postage stamps of perhaps more picturesque design and varied colours.

GK's Weekly, 5 November 1927

THE WAY TO LOVE

All pessimism has a secret optimism for its object. All surrender of life, all denial of pleasure, all darkness, all austerity, has for its real aim this separation of something so that it may be poignantly and perfectly enjoyed . . . The way to love anything is to realize that it might be lost.

Tremendous Trifles, London 1909

VICKY BOYS

We never called ourselves Victorians while we really were Victorians.

The Illustrated London News, 30 May 1936

CARRIED AWAY

The moderns do not realize modernity. They have never known anything else. They have stepped on to a moving platform which they hardly know to be moving . . .

The Illustrated London News, 14 March 1931

MONKEYING ABOUT

The Dean of St Paul's [Dean Inge], when he is right, is very right. He is right with all that ringing emphasis that makes him in other matters so rashly and disastrously wrong. And I cannot but hail with gratitude the scorn with which he spoke lately of all the newspaper nonsense about using monkey-glands to turn old men into young men . . .*

The Thing, New York 1930

*W. Somerset Maugham, born in the same year as GKC, took this treatment. He died at 91; GKC at 62.

LINGUA FRANCA

Probably we have never properly explained [to the critics of Roman Catholicism] the real case for using Latin for something that must be immutable and universal. But as half of them are howling day and night for an international language, and accepting a journalese jibberish with plurals in 'oj' because they can get no better, some glimmering of the old use of Latin by Erasmus or Bacon might reasonably be expected of them.

The Thing, New York 1930

NOT PYGMALION LIKELY

There was a rumour recently that the 'Pygmalion' of Mr Bernard Shaw was to be filmed. It was, I think, unauthorized; but it is strange that it should be even reported. To talk of seeing 'Pygmalion' on the cinema is like talking of having heard the Venus de Milo on the trombone . . . The whole point of 'Pygmalion' consists in words being pronounced in a particular accent, and you can no more film an accent than you can carve a tune or sing a statue . . .*

The Illustrated London News, 19 June 1920

*GKC was of course writing in the time of silent films; when the 'talkies' came in, *My Fair Lady* was a huge success.

GABUNDANT

. . . It is always the humble man who talks too much; the proud man watches himself too closely.

The Man Who Was Thursday, London 1908

PROVENANCE UNKNOWN

'Nobody knows where anything comes from nowadays, Douglas,' said Braintree quietly. 'That's what's called publicity and popular journalism in a capitalist state. My tie may be made by capitalists; so may yours be made by cannibal islanders for all you know.'

'Woven out of the whiskers of missionaries,' replied Murrel. 'A pleasant thought . . .'

The Return of Don Quixote, London 1927

DIET OF WORMS

[Murrel:] 'Yes, of course I know him. I don't think anybody knows him very well.'

'Sort of book-worm, I suppose,' observed Archer.

'Well, we're all worms,' remarked Murrel cheerfully. 'I suppose a book-worm shows a rather refined and superior taste in diet . . .'

The Return of Don Quixote, London 1927

THAT'S THE WAY TO DO IT

. . . The cinema prevails over Punch and Judy not as great art, but merely as big business. There was probably more fun got out of Punch and Judy, but there was less money got out of it.

The Illustrated London News, 8 October 1921

GKC adds: '. . . Do not our day-dreams of practical politics now largely consist in wishing we could hit wooden heads with a wooden stick?'

THE INSULAR FRENCH

It is not only truism but tautology to say that the people of our island have been insular; yet the fine shade and peril of that insularity have never been understood. In one sense people are more insular when they are not islanders. The French travel much less than the English; they concentrate on their own nation with what seems to some a narrow nationalism. It was expressed by the great Balzac when he suggested that Frenchmen stay at home because nothing is better than France while Englishmen travel because anything is better than England.

The Illustrated London News, 6 October 1923

PROPHETS OF DOOM

The prophet of woe, whenever he is really a true prophet, is always trying to be a false prophet. The prophet could not utter his prophecies except in order to falsify his prophecies. If I say that England may become pagan and servile, it is naturally in the hope that she may prefer to become Christian and free.

The Illustrated London News, 1 September 1923

COULEUR DE ROSE

Pink is the withering of the rose and the fading of the fire; pink is mere anaemia in the blood of the universe.

'About Shirts', *As I Was Saying*, London 1936

THE GROTESQUE

. . . All grotesqueness is itself intimately related to seriousness. Unless a thing is dignified, it cannot be undignified. Why is it funny that a man should sit down suddenly in the street? There is only one possible or intelligent reason: that man is the image of God.

'Spiritualism', *All Things Considered*, London 1908

MODERNISM

The real objection to modernism is simply that it is a form of snobbishness. It is an attempt to crush a rational opponent not by reason, but by some mystery of superiority, by hinting that one is specially up to date or particularly 'in the know' . . . To introduce into philosophical discussions a sneer at a creed's antiquity is like introducing a sneer at a lady's age. It is caddish because it is irrelevant.

'The Case for the Ephemeral', *All Things Considered*, London 1908

ECONOMICAL WITH THE *ACTUALITÉ*

There is no great harm in the theorist who makes up a new theory to fit a new event. But the theorist who starts with a false theory and then sees everything as making it come true is the most dangerous enemy of human reason.

The Flying Inn, London 1914

WHO'S RESPONSIBLE?

The question for brave men is not whether a certain thing is increasing; the question is whether we are increasing it.

'Woman', *All Things Considered*, London 1908

WHAT MORRIS ACHIEVED

The great achievement of William Morris was this: that he nearly convinced a whole generation that the nineteenth century was not normal. In this he was years and years ahead of the Communists of the twentieth century, who still really believe that the nineteenth century was normal.

The Illustrated London News, 17 March 1934

NOVEL THOUGHTS, NOVEL IDEAS

I should like to ask in all humility why it is that novelists talk nonsense when they begin to theorize, or, in other words, to think? . . . I mean by thinking, ordinary thinking; putting two and two together and not thinking they make three. I mean not contradicting flatly at the end of a sentence what you have stated positively at the start.

The Illustrated London News, 21 April 1928

He goes on to attack the American novelist Theodore Dreiser.

ULTERIOR MOTIVE

I fear it is more often the motive that creates the argument than the argument that creates the motive.

The Illustrated London News, 24 April 1926

PROPHET MARGINS

The one really rousing thing about human history is that, whether or no the proceedings go right, at any rate the prophecies always go wrong . . . Even when good things do happen, they are never the good things that were guaranteed. And even when bad things happen, they are never the bad things that were inevitable.

The Illustrated London News, 17 April 1926

NOT FIT TO BROADCAST

GKC was writing about 'the absurdity of talking about listening-in to spectacles which are obviously for the eye and not for the ear'.

When a paper announced, 'listening-in to the launching of a ship', it might just as well talk about 'Smelling a Famous Statue' or 'Special Seats to View the Taste of Garlic'.

The Illustrated London News, 7 May 1927

QUEL DOMMAGE!

It takes all sorts to make a world; and France has not produced a Shakespeare or a nonsense rhyme.

The Illustrated London News, 26 March 1927

THE (UNWRITTEN) BRITISH CONSTITUTION

. . . Saying 'We may not understand political theories, but our constitution works well in practice', is a piece of wild paradox and only loved as such, like a nonsense rhyme of Lear or Lewis Carroll. It is exactly like saying: 'We cannot add up figures correctly; we are quite content if the result comes out right.'

The Illustrated London News, 26 March 1927

THE VALUE OF FOOLS

There is a certain solid use in fools. It is not so much that they rush in where angels fear to tread, but rather that they let out what devils intend to do. Some perversion of folly will float about nameless and pervade a whole society; then some lunatic gives it a name, and henceforth it is harmless. With all really evil things, when the danger has appeared the danger is over.

'The Futurists', *Alarms and Discursions*, London 1911

GOING FOR A SONG

I can remember that my own grandfather thought it perfectly natural to have Community Singing. Only he did not call it Community Singing. He called it singing. He thought it as natural as eating and drinking and talking and laughing. All these five things generally went together.

The Illustrated London News, 19 February 1927

GKC was amused that somebody who said he went in for Community Singing was sourly told, 'Why don't you go to Russia?' by someone else who thought he meant Communist singing.

THE BOY NEXT DOOR

We make our friends; we make our enemies; but God makes our next-door neighbour. Hence he comes to us clad in all the careless terrors of nature: he is as strange as the stars, as reckless and indifferent as the rain. He is Man, the most terrible of the beasts. That is why the old religions and the old scriptural language showed so sharp a wisdom when they spoke, not of one's duty towards humanity, but one's duty towards one's neighbour.

Heretics, London 1906

FAMILY

It is a good thing for a man to live in a family for the same reason that it is a good thing for a man to be besieged in a city. It is a good idea for a man to live in a family in the same sense that it is a beautiful and delightful thing for a man to be snowed up in a street. They all force him to realize that life is not a thing from outside, but a thing from inside.

Heretics, London 1906

BURNING ISSUE

It is foolish, generally speaking, for a philosopher to set fire to another philosopher in Smithfield Market because they do not agree in their theory of the universe. That was done very frequently in the last decadence of the Middle Ages, and it failed altogether in its object. But there is one thing that is infinitely more absurd and unpractical than burning a man for his philosophy. This is the habit of saying that his philosophy does not matter, and this is done universally in the twentieth century . . .

Heretics, London 1906

MADNESS

Every one who has had the misfortune to talk with people in the heart or on the edge of mental disorder, knows that their most sinister quality is a horrible clarity of detail; a connecting of one thing with another in a map more elaborate than a maze. If you argue with a madman, it is extremely probable that you will get the worst of it; for in many ways his mind moves all the quicker for not being delayed by the things that go with good judgement.

Orthodoxy, London 1909

CURING THE INSANE

[With the mad] every remedy is a desperate remedy. Every cure is a miraculous cure. Curing a madman is not arguing with a philosopher; it is casting out a devil.

Orthodoxy, London 1909

WIT'S END

. . . As all thoughts and theories were once judged by whether they tended to make a man lose his soul . . . all modern thoughts and theories may be judged by whether they tend to make a man lose his wits.

Orthodoxy, London 1909

AN ENGLISHMAN'S HOME IS HIS CASTLE

I for one should love to have a real moat round my house, with a little drawbridge which could be let down when I really like the look of the visitor.

The Illustrated London News, 26 September 1925

A NATURAL MISTAKE

We all have a little weakness, which is very natural but rather misleading, for supposing that this epoch must be the end of the world because it will be the end of us.

The Illustrated London News, 15 August 1925

PRISON REFORM

There is great talk of better conditions in prisons, like better conditions in stables; cleaner water or purer air. But at the bottom of their hearts, or at least at the back of their minds, these humanitarians think it as natural that poor people should be in prison as that horses should be in stables.

The Illustrated London News, 22 August 1925

IN MY END IS MY BEGINNING

It is only when great societies come to an end, like antiquity or the *ancien régime*, that men can see them as a whole and realize what was seeking to destroy them and why.

The Illustrated London News, 4 July 1925

NASTY COMPLAINTS

Father Brown: 'People who complain are just jolly, human Christian nuisances; I don't mind them. But people who complain that they never complain are the devil. They are really the devil; isn't that swagger of stoicism the whole point of the Byronic cult of Satan?'

'The Actor and the Alibi' (*The Father Brown Stories*)

TOO CLOSE FOR COMFORT

'There is one general truth to remember,' said Father Brown . . . 'A thing can sometimes be too close to be seen; as, for instance, a man cannot see himself. There was a man who had a fly in his eye when he looked through the telescope, and he discovered that there was a most incredible dragon on the moon.'

'The Song of the Flying Fish' (*The Father Brown Stories*)

THE MIND IS A DOTTED LINE

'Recent experiments', went on the professor, quietly, 'have suggested that our consciousness is not continuous, but is a succession of very rapid impressions like a cinema . . . The mind is not a continuous line, but rather a dotted line.'

'The Miracle of Moon Crescent' (*The Father Brown Stories*)

GIVE ME A BELL

I am just old enough to remember the world before telephones. And I remember that my father and my uncle fitted up the first telephone I ever saw with their own metal and chemicals, a miniature telephone reaching from the top bedroom under the roof to the remote end of the garden. I was really impressed imaginatively by this; and I do not think I have ever been so much impressed since by any extension of it. The point is rather important in the whole theory of imagination. It did startle me that a voice should sound in the room when it was really as distant as the next street. It would hardly have startled me more if it had been as distant as the next town. It does not startle me any more if it is as distant as the next continent. The miracle is over.

The Illustrated London News, 8 February 1930

GOLD FISH

The soul of Mr Peregrine Smart hovered like a fly round one possession and one joke. It might be considered a mild joke, for it consisted merely of asking people if they had seen his goldfish . . .

The peculiar thing about the goldfish was that they were made of gold. They were part of an eccentric but expensive toy, said to have been made by the freak of some rich Eastern prince, and Mr Smart had picked it up at some sale or in some curiosity shop, such as he frequented for the purpose of lumbering up his house with unique and useless things.

'The Song of the Flying Fish' (*The Father Brown Stories*)

POETS

'I don't deny', [Innocent Smith] said, 'that there should be priests to remind men that they will one day die. I only say that at certain strange epochs it is necessary to have another kind of priests, called poets, actually to remind men that they are not dead yet.'

Manalive, 1915

MODEST CLAIMS

We . . . have considerable belief in the power of powerful understatement. It is the power which in the past belonged to good manners, and in the present is chiefly contradicted by advertisement. A host recommending his wine does it in a different way from a huckster recommending his latest substitute for wine . . . And if the host's wine should turn out to be really good, or better than he suggested, we shall probably think it even better than it is.

GK's Weekly, 15 January 1927

LAW OF THE LETTER

. . . The first and most obvious method [of standardizing correspondence] would be for the Government to send round official forms for our family correspondence, to be filled up like the forms about Insurance or Income Tax. Here and there, even in the most model communication, there would be words left blank which the individual might be allowed to supply for himself. I have a half-formed ideal of an official love-letter, printed in the manner of 'I _____ you' so that the citizen might insert 'love', or 'like', or 'adore', with a view to the new civil marriage; or 'renounce', or 'repudiate', or 'execrate' with a view to yet newer and more civil divorce.

The Illustrated London News, 30 July 1921

BEGGING NOT TO DIFFER

. . . The nicer sort of crank is rare. And the difficulty about him is not that he differs from everybody else, but that he cannot believe that anybody else differs from him. He thinks things are self-evident which are really in the last degree questionable; and he thinks opinions are universal which the mass of mankind has never heard of. He labours under the fixed idea that you and I do not know what our opinions are and he kindly explains them to us.

The Illustrated London News, 19 July 1913

FORGET IT!

Do not talk about good old times or bad old times. There never were any old times. If a friend says to you, 'Are you better?' you do not say, 'Better than I was at thirteen; slightly worse than I was at sixteen; gravely worse than I was at eighteen; but immensely better than I was at twenty-three.' You talk about yesterday; or, better still, about today.

The Illustrated London News, 4 October 1913

SMASHING TIME

Human codes are faulty, like human clocks. But to smash all the clocks and then say, dogmatically, 'You never can tell the time', affects me as unreasonable.

The Illustrated London News, 29 November 1913

MANY HAPPY RETURNS

Christmas is quite certainly the most interesting thing in England today. It is the last living link between all that remains of the most delicate religious devotion and all that exists of the coarsest town vulgarity . . . The return of old things in new times, by an established and automatic machinery, is the permanent security of men who like to be sane. The greatest of all blessings is the boomerang. And all the healthier things we know are boomerangs – that is, they are things that return. Sleep is a boomerang. We fling it from us at morning, and it knocks us down again at night . . . To have such an institution as Christmas is, I will not say to make an accident inevitable, but I will say to make an adventure recurrent – and therefore, in one sense, to make an adventure everlasting.

The Illustrated London News, 20 December 1913

FORGIVE OUR FOOLISH WAYS

A knave, by his vices, is dangerous. A fool, by his virtues, may sometimes be still more dangerous.

The Illustrated London News, 15 March 1913

NO TRUE COMPROMISE

A political compromise is like two children tugging at a cracker till it comes in two in the middle. One child gets one half, but the other half flies away.

The Illustrated London News, 23 July 1910

TAILPIECE

A dog is a sort of curly tail to a man; a substitute for that which man so tragically lost at an early stage of evolution. And though I would rather myself go about trailing a dog behind me than tugging a pianola or towing a rose-garden, yet this is a matter of taste, and they are alike appendages or things dependent upon man.

The Illustrated London News, 2 July 1910

VIVE LA FRANCE

The Marseillaise once sounded like the human voice of the volcano or the dance-tune of the earthquake; and the kings of the earth trembled; some fearing that the heavens might fall; some fearing far more that justice might be done. The Marseillaise is played today at diplomatic dinner-parties, where smiling monarchs meet beaming millionaires, and is rather less revolutionary than 'Home, Sweet Home'.

St Thomas Aquinas, London 1933

THE INEPT SAVAGE

Savagery has many vices and some virtues; but it has, above all, the great virtue of inefficiency.

The Illustrated London News, 6 August 1910

A WINE DISTINCTION

The dipsomaniac and the abstainer are not only both mistaken, but they both make the same mistake. They both regard wine as a drug and not as a drink.

George Bernard Shaw, London 1910

VANITY AND PRIDE

Vanity means thinking somebody's praise important, more important than yourself. But pride . . . is thinking yourself more important than anything that can praise or blame you.

The Illustrated London News, 29 October 1910

THE ETERNAL TRIANGLE

The tendency of mankind to split up everything into three is hard to explain rationally. It is either false and a piece of superstition; or it is true and a part of religion. In either case it cannot be adequately explained on ordinary human judgement or average human experience. Three is really a very uncommon number in nature. The dual principle runs through nature as a whole; it is almost as if our Earth and heaven had been made by the Heavenly Twins. There is no beast with three horns; no bird with three wings; no fish with three fins and no more . . . Yet [Man with his curious taste for the number three] shows it in everything from the Three Brothers in the fairy-tale to the Three Estates of the realm; in everything from the Three Dimensions to the Three Bears. If the thing has a reason, it must be a reason beyond reason.

The Illustrated London News, 26 November 1910

CHRISTMAS CARDS

A large liberty, and even licence, may be permitted to Christmas cards. It takes all sorts to make a world, and vulgarity at least does not tend to *unmake* the world, as do some forms of refinement. For my part, I am a fastidious critic in this matter. I demand for myself a proper Christmas card that is about

Christmas. I demand (such is my artistic exclusiveness) a picture of a plum-pudding with legs running away from a pursuing mince-pie. At the very least my critical sense requires a couple of frosted robins, with white spangly stuff on the top of a cottage-roof . . .

The Illustrated London News, 24 December 1910

YOURS SINCERELY

We do not (at least, I do not) respect any sect, Church or group because of its sincerity. Sincerity merely means actuality. It only means that a man's opinion undoubtedly is his opinion. But if a man's opinion is that he ought to burn dogs alive, I do not respect him because he really feels like that; on the contrary, I should respect him more if I could believe that it was an elegant affectation.

The Illustrated London News, 15 October 1910

TYPE-CASTING

Through all my own dreams, especially waking dreams, there run and caper and collide only four characters, who seem to sum up the four ultimate types of our existence. These four figures are: St George and the Dragon, and the Princess offered to the Dragon, and the Princess's father, who was (if I remember right) the King of Egypt. You have everything in those figures: active virtue destroying evil; passive virtue enduring evil; ignorance or convention permitting evil; and Evil.

The Illustrated London News, 15 October 1910

I VOW TO ME

The man who makes a vow makes an appointment with himself at some distant time or place. The danger of it is that himself should not keep the appointment.

The Defendant, London 1901

REVOLUTIONARY OPTIMISTS

Every one of the great revolutionists, from Isaiah to Shelley, have been optimists. They have been indignant, not about the badness of existence, but about the slowness of men in realizing its goodness.

The Defendant, London 1901

THE CHIMAERA

The Greeks . . . committed us to a horrible asceticism – the worship of the aesthetic type alone . . . The chimaera was a creature of whom any healthy-minded people would have been proud; but when we see it in Greek pictures, we feel inclined to tie a ribbon round its neck and give it a saucer of milk.

The Defendant, London 1901

WINTERLUDE

Some little time ago I stood among immemorial English trees that seemed to take hold upon the stars like a brood of Ygdrasils. As I walked among these living pillars I became gradually aware that the rustics who lived and died in their shadow adopted a very curious conversational tone. They seemed to be constantly apologising for the trees, as if they were a very poor show. After elaborate investigation I discovered that their gloomy and penitent tone was traceable to the fact that it was winter and all the trees were bare. I assured them that I did not resent the fact that it was winter, that I knew the thing had happened before, and that no foresight on their part could have averted this blow of destiny. But I could not reconcile them to the fact that it *was* winter. There was evidently a general feeling that I had caught the trees in a kind of disgraceful deshabille, and that they ought not to be seen until, like the first human sinners, they had covered themselves in leaves.

The Defendant, London 1901

WITH ALL DUE RESPECT

What precisely do people mean when they talk about 'respecting other people's opinions'? I do not mean that they mean nothing; I really want to know what they mean. I understand respecting the other people; I understand what it means when it says in the Bible, 'Honour all men.' For men have certain capacities or functions which are noble in themselves, and cannot be wholly abdicated. Just as there is some importance attaching to Nero merely as an Emperor, so there is some importance attaching to Nero merely as a man . . . We might hit a millionaire, or even kill him, but we must not chain him upon a kennel. It would insult mankind. I might vote for an eminent banker's execution, or even assist in his assassination; but I would not put him between the shafts of my hansom-cab . . . because I should then be insulting him as a man and not as a tyrant or a usurer. I should be insulting myself as well as him.

The Illustrated London News, 15 October 1910

GRIM GRIN

. . . However much my face clouds with sombre vanity, or vulgar vengeance, or contemptible contempt, the bones of my skull beneath it are laughing for ever.

The Defendant, London 1901

FOR PITY'S SAKE

I think the Anti-Vivisectionists are right . . . It may be unreasonable to say, 'Love me, love my dog.' I do not think it so unreasonable to say, 'Pity my dog, or you will lose the habit of pitying me.'

The Illustrated London News, 3 May 1913

IRISH STOOGE

All the real amiability which most Englishmen feel towards Irishmen is lavished upon a class of Irishmen which unfortunately does not exist. The Irishman of the English farce, with his brogue, his buoyancy, and his tender-hearted irresponsibility, is a man who ought to have been thoroughly pampered with praise and sympathy, if he had only existed to receive them. Unfortunately, all the time that we were creating a comic Irishman in fiction, we were creating a tragic Irishman in fact.

George Bernard Shaw, London 1910

HUMBLE PI

The act of defending any of the cardinal virtues has today all the exhilaration of a vice . . . And especially . . . there is about one who defends humility something inexpressibly rakish.

The Defendant, London 1901

INDEX

The way I have indexed the GKC gobbets is to give the page number followed by the first three letters of the gobbet's heading. When two gobbets on one page begin with the same three, or more, letters, I have added letters until the two are differentiated from each other – BH.

Index

Index

Napoleon Bonaparte 102PRE, 102FAG, 112GRE
Nationalization 100CHA, 243INT
Native Americans 135HIA, 139–40DIC
Nature 18NOR, 216CAT
neighbours 14NIG, 15BRE, 85SUB, 251THE
Nero, Emperor 263WIT
newspapers: *see* 'journalism'
New Witness, The xxxviii
Nietzsche, Friedrich 16IFY, 76HEA
Nihilists 5NIH
Noel, Revd Conrad xxxiii
nonsense 1THE, 230PAN
novels 68–9NOV, 70HIS, 136AME, 206OFF
novelists 249NOV
nudists 151GAN
nursery rhymes 61NUR

obscurity 62OBS
obstacles 219OBS
O'Casey, Sean xxvii–xxviii
occupations 128WELL
O'Connor, Father John xxxix
oddity 240ODD
Odin 124SNO
old age 233NOR
Old Wives' Tales 23OLD
opposition 204UPP
optimist, the 218THE
oratory 106–7JOS
ordeal 79–80CAN
originality 237MOM
original sin 166ORI
orthodoxy 172JUM
Orwell, George xix, xx, xxiii
ostrich 211INC
Oxford 154OXB
Oxford Union Society xv

Pacifists 219PAC
paganism 173SEE, 186THE
pain 236PAI
Palmer, Mary Louise (Mrs Jack Hillier) x
panic 230PAN
paradox in GKC xxviii, xxix
paradoxes 199PAR
Paris 209ETE, 219–20GAR

Parliament 214BRO
Parnell, Charles 190ACI
parting 28SUC
past, the 9PAS
Pater, Walter xxxii, 51WAL
peacemaker 5PAX
pedestrians 81FOO
penny dreadfuls 69PEN
perversion 64–5PER
pessimism 52–3HARDYSPE, 228ANS, 243THE
Peter Pan 53–4PET
Peter, St 171STP
philosophers 252BUR
photography 8THE *and see* 'colour photography'
Picasso, Pablo 88–9IMP
picnic 224IND
pink 247COU
Pio Nono: *see* 'Pius IX, Pope'
Piper, John xxvii
pirates 2WAL, 212PIR
pistol 3BAN
Pius IX, Pope 178PIO
Plato 39COL
pleasure 236PAI
Poe, Edgar Allan 43–4POE
poet, idea of 42–3TEN, 70THEB
Poet Laureate 66THE
poetry 37WIL, 62WHA, 68MOD, 237THE
poets 32ROM, 70THEB, 255–6POE
poisons 165ONE
Poland 210ASP
police 201POL
politicians 227IGN
politics 227IGN
poor, the 153EDUCATIN
Pope, Alexander 68SHA
Pope, the 127SIG
Popper, (Sir) Karl 202BEWn
popularity 67YOU
pork 175–6PIG
practical jokes: *see* 'jokes'
prayer 180ONP, 184THEB
predestination 37WIL
prejudices 168DOD, 235PRE
press, the: *see* 'journalism'
press gang, the 102PRE
pride 260VAN
primitive man 27ALW

prisons 253PRI
privacy 62–3PRI
profanity 231–2PRO
Prohibition 16ONA, 133PRO, 134MOR, 134–5BLA
property 204PRO
prophecies 199PRO, 247PRO, 249PRO
prostitution 204PRO
Protestantism 180–1THE, 196DID
Protestants 57HIL, 181THEA
psychoanalysis 7HID, 21SOT
psychology 116ENGLISHPS, 239THE
public house 224THE
public relations 211PUB
Punch 57HIL
Punch and Judy 246THA
Puritanism 170CRO, 174PUR, 174TOO
Puritans 137–8THE, 138THA, 167SUP, 183NEV, 197NOP
Pygmalion 245NOT

Quakers 176ACC, 196STA
quarrel 5PAX
quizzes 83QUI

railways 156CAR
raw umber 22UMB
reason (for) 21THE
Red Indians: *see* 'Native Americans'
Red Queen 18–19ITS
Redway (publisher) xxxiii
reflections 182REF
reformers 15ZEA
relativity 18–19ITS
religion 181–2THEH, 188–9ATE, 194SOM, 196STA
religion and science 114SCI
religions 191BEG
Republicans (American) 139POS
respect 263WIT
resurrection 177RIS
revolt 144NOK
revolutionists 262REV
rhyme 51RHY, 65–6RHY, 66ANA
Richard II, King 42ANO

Index

Index

★(Footnote to page 215) I am grateful to M. Raymond-Josué Seckel of the Bibliothèque nationale de France, who at a late proof stage of this book kindly supplied this information about (François Louis) Emile Baube (b. 1865): he did not become a *deputé*, but stood in the Paris legislative elections of 6 May 1906, describing himself as a candidate for the 'Comite républicain socialiste, anti-collectiviste, antiministériel' – which is close to what GKC writes. Baube was beaten in the first round by (Gabriel) Auguste Failliot (1851–1922), who was elected for the first district of the fourth *arrondissement*. (See *Le Figaro*, 7 May 1906 and *Le Temps*, 8 May 1906.) By profession, Baube was an industrialist involved in the manufacture of perfumes.

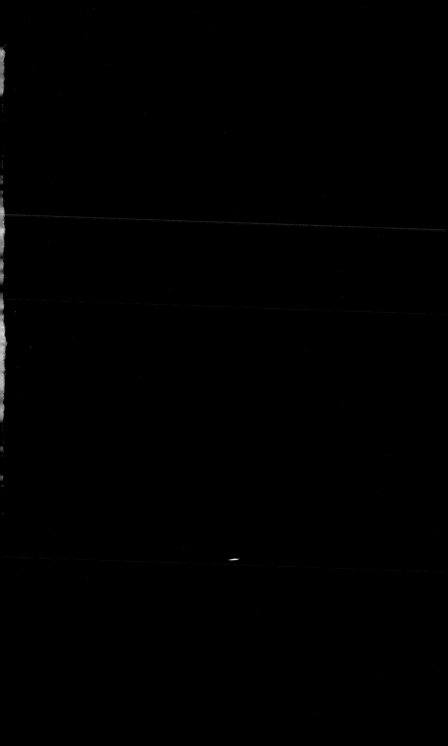